FABRIC Blooms

42 Flowers to Make, Wear & Adorn Your Life

Megan Hunt

LARK

LARK

An Imprint of Sterling Publishing
387 Park Avenue South
New York, NY 10016

ISBN 978-1-4547-0801-8

Library of Congress Cataloging-in-Publication Data

Hunt, Megan.
  Fabric blooms : 42 flowers to make, wear & adorn your life / Megan Hunt.
      pages cm
  Includes index.
  ISBN 978-1-4547-0801-8
  1. Fabric flowers. I. Title.
  TT890.5.H86 2013
  745.594'3—dc23
          2013027461

Distributed in Canada by Sterling Publishing
c/o Canadian Manda Group, 165 Dufferin Street
Toronto, Ontario, Canada M6K 3H6
Distributed in the United Kingdom by GMC Distribution Services
Castle Place, 166 High Street, Lewes, East Sussex, England BN7 1XU
Distributed in Australia by Capricorn Link (Australia) Pty. Ltd.
P.O. Box 704, Windsor, NSW 2756, Australia

For information about custom editions, special sales, and premium and corporate purchases, please
contact Sterling Special Sales at 800-805-5489 or specialsales@sterlingpublishing.com.

Email academic@larkbooks.com for information about desk and examination copies.
The complete policy can be found at larkcrafts.com.
Every effort has been made to ensure that all the information in this book is accurate. However, due
to differing conditions, tools, and individual skills, the publisher cannot be responsible for any injuries,
losses, and other damages that may result from the use of the information in this book.

Manufactured in China

2 4 6 8 10 9 7 5 3 1

larkcrafts.com

≪CONTENTS≫

To Wear

At Home

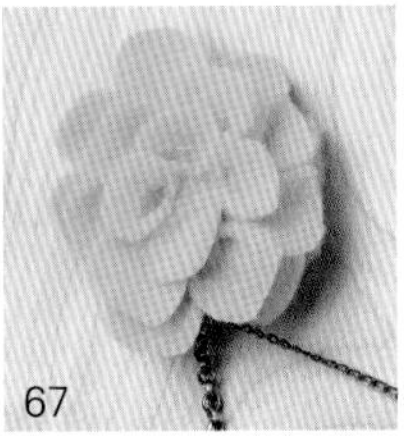
67

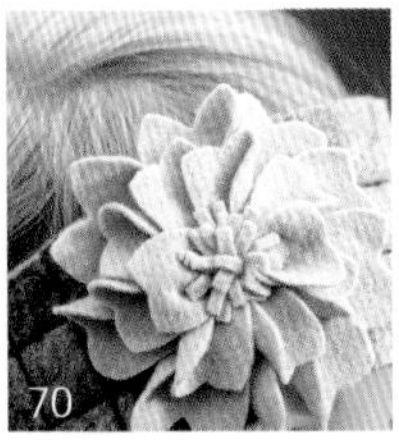
70

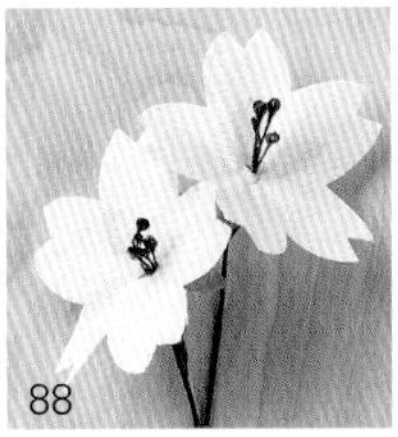
88

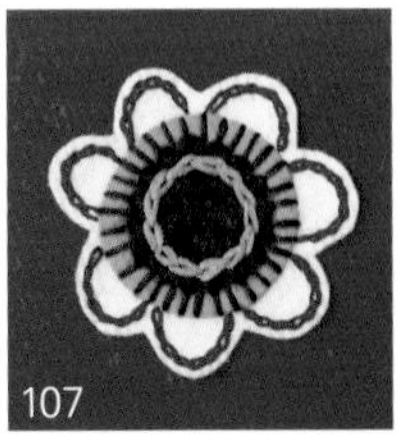
107

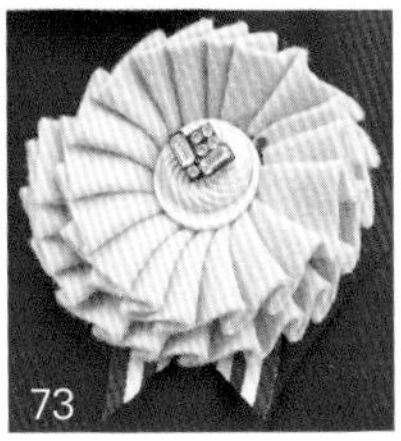
73

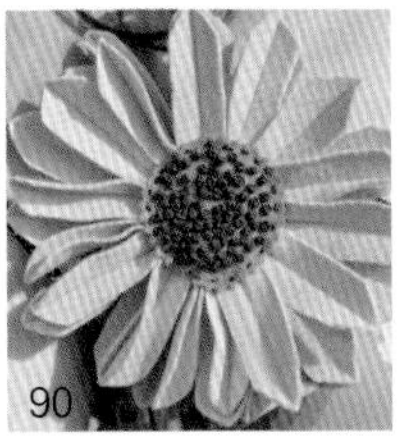
90

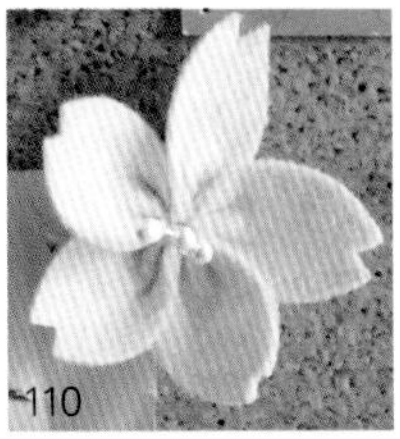
110

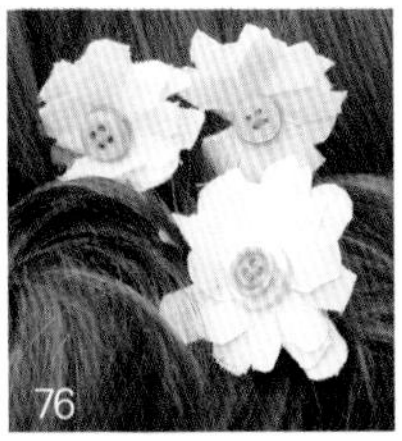
76

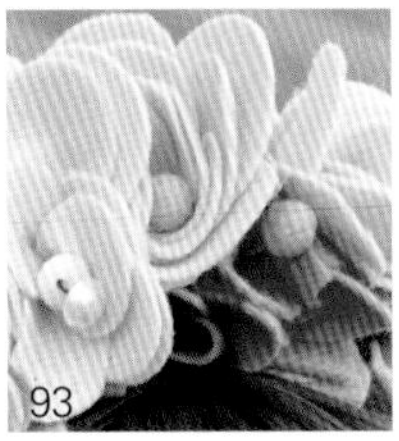
93

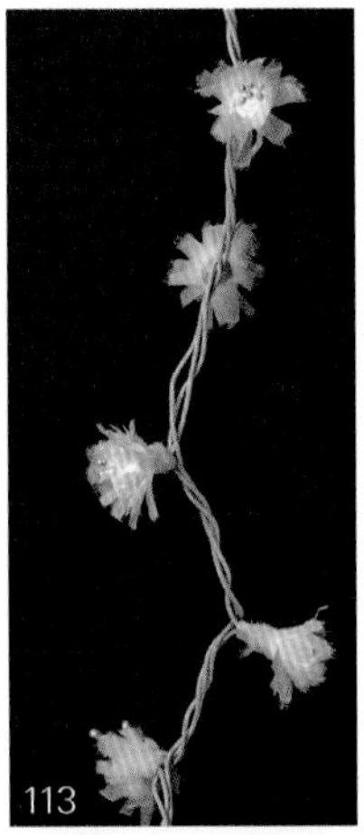
113

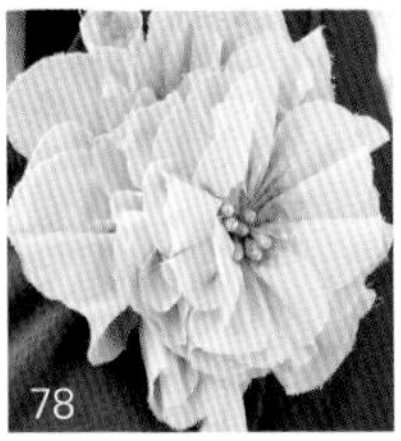
78

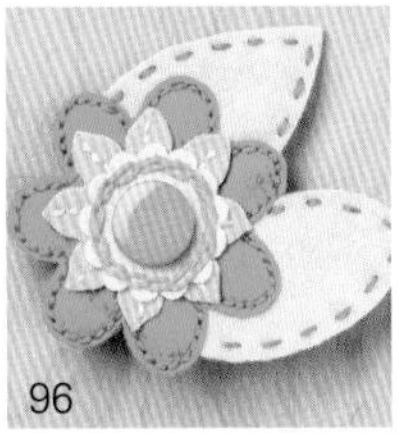
96

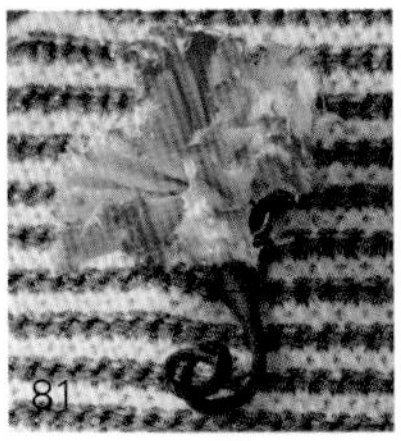
81

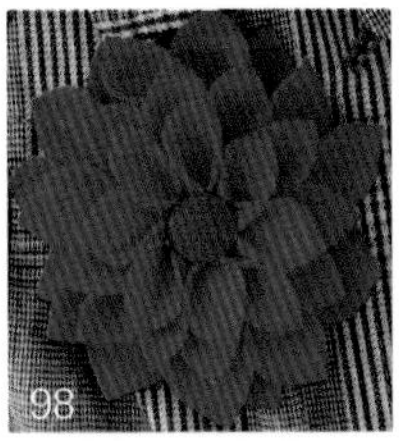
98

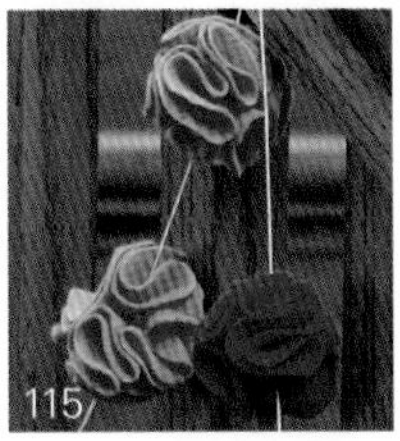
115

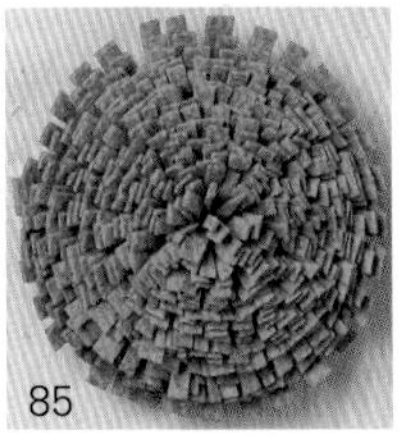
85

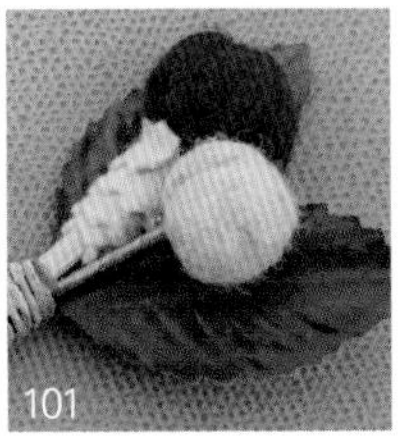
101

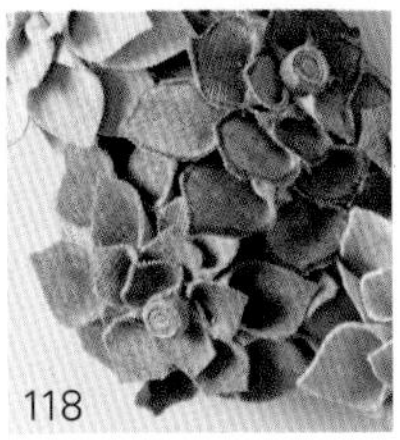
118

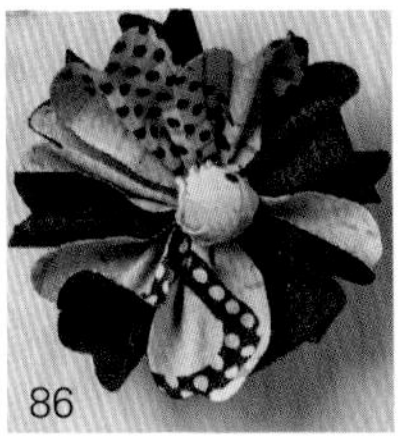
86

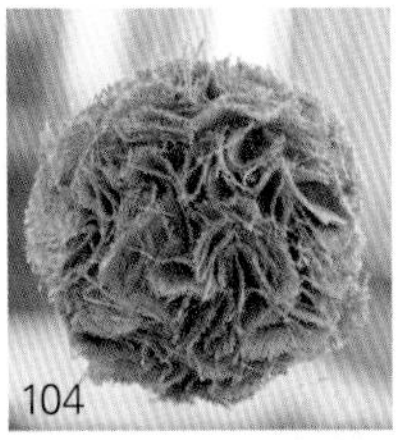
104

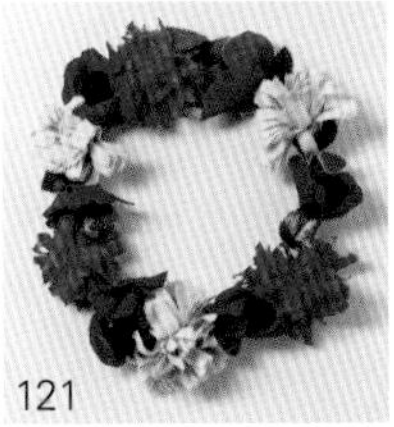
121

≪INTRODUCTION≫

HI, THERE. MY NAME IS MEGAN and I am a project designer, writer, and over-sharer, and I like to think of myself as a good friend, too. In 2005, I started a small business using fabric, felt, embroidery, and vintage buttons to create bouquets and flowers for weddings called Princess Lasertron. As my company grew, I added consulting and a line of bridesmaid and wedding dresses to my list of offerings, but even now, my favorite projects are still the flowers. Creating an heirloom bouquet for a bride, exchanging emails and packages full of inspiration and small family treasures to integrate into each design, and seeing my work in the photos from a couple's biggest milestone together are the most special and rewarding things about my job. For several years, I've enjoyed the honor of working with each individual bride to translate her vision for her wedding flowers into reality, and I'm so excited to now be able to share all of my techniques and methods in this book.

Fast-forward to this moment! I have been busy for the past year carefully recording each step-by-step process for all of my favorite flowers, as well as coming up with some new designs exclusively for this book. In these pages, you'll find 42 easy flowers designed for beginning crafters, and if plunking a stem in a vase isn't your thing, I've got you covered with plenty of projects inspired by each pretty bloom. From sweater clips to hair clips, and from wreaths to throw pillows (why not?), there are endless ways to enjoy the tradition of flower making while retaining a modern aesthetic that you'll love to have in your home or wardrobe.

Most of the flowers use very easy-to-source materials, so you can get that quick gratification of finishing a project you made yourself. I designed these projects to be perfect for a rainy day with your niece, to find something cool to do with your pretty vintage fabric, or to give you the skills to whip out a quick birthday gift for a friend. No matter what your style is, I think you'll find these simple projects to be a great jumping-off point for creating something truly your own.

Now for a word on the types of projects you'll find here and how to navigate them. Personally, I've always been one to dive right into a project and figure things out as I go, resulting in some of my more "Regretsy-worthy" moments as a crafter. For this reason, I've provided plenty of visual instructions and photographs for each project

to help you discover your own process as you work. Whether you're a rule-follower or a skimmer, these projects will offer you inspiration and motivation to pick up your scissors and make something!

I hope this book helps you develop skills and techniques that inspire and connect you to the deep and rich tradition of flower making: the satisfying snip through a piece of fabric; the tug of thread as you draw back a stitch; the texture and weight of vintage buttons collected over the years, sitting in a bowl on your desk just waiting for the perfect home on a frothy, newly fabricated blossom.

Explore your creative potential with the materials you have, assemble some simple supplies, and bring a little more beauty into the world.

BASICS

We all have our trusty tools of the trade, and these are my indispensable crafting tools when it comes to flower making. Many of them may be things you have on hand if you are already an avid crafter, and all of them are easily sourced from local craft and hobby stores. I encourage you to search around online or in vintage stores for unique findings, fabrics, and other frivolities that will give your flowers a personal life of their own.

Findings

Keep your eyes out for items like hair clips, headband blanks, brooch pin backs, shoe clips, etc. Whenever I see these things on sale or get a coupon to use, you can bet I'll be filling up my stash of these findings for beautiful, wearable flower gifts and accessories. Having the right notions on hand will change the fate of a flower forever!

Fabrics

Making a flower doesn't usually take a lot of fabric, so it's the perfect time to dig into your stash of remnants and scraps. I also love repurposing fabric from vintage clothing and linens, especially delicate, threadbare cottons. Those "vintage-y" lightweight weaves and faded pastels are perfect for making flower petals. Here are the most common fabrics I use when making flowers.

Felt
I like to buy wool felt by the yard so I can work with large pieces at a time. It can be tricky to source 100% wool felt yardage, but you may be able to find wool blends at your local fabric store in a limited selection of colors. I buy

my yardage online at woolfeltcentral.com. The ladies who run that site are wonderfully accommodating and helpful. Online auction sites and Etsy.com are other good places to start a search for good-quality felt yardage. Felt is my favorite material to work with because it's so easy to sew, doesn't unravel, and lends itself well to embellishment.

Cotton
Cotton is durable and very stable, making it perfect for a variety of creative projects. It washes and dyes easily, and it's one of the most readily available fabrics, whether you're searching in your local craft store or your own closet for clothing you can repurpose.

Cotton Lawn
Cotton lawn is a delicate, finely-woven fabric that is perfect for making soft flower petals. The fabric is not quite sheer, and it's best to use a small needle and fine cotton thread when working with it to keep the weave intact. It also takes well to light iron-on interfacing for when you want the beautiful look of cotton lawn with a little bit more strength.

Jersey
Jersey is a knit fabric with lots of stretch, and it won't unravel when you cut it. It also feels like a more casual fabric to me, which is great when you want to make a project that doesn't feel too fancy. Fabric stiffener works well on cotton-knit jersey, and it's easy to iron and crease, which is important when manipulating the material to create petals and folds.

Faux Leather

I love to opt for cruelty-free materials, and faux leather can easily be found in craft and hobby stores or online in a variety of textures and colors. Called PU or "pleather," faux leather is easier to sew and cut than the real thing. This material will tend to wear out your needles more quickly, though, so always keep plenty of new sharps handy. I also recommend tracing templates on the wrong side of the fabric and using a pressing cloth to protect the fabric if you choose to iron it.

Thread

Every crafter worth her scissors stash has a preferred thread, and mine is embroidery floss. It's the thread equivalent of a permanent marker, drawing satisfyingly thick lines across your fabric canvas. I love the ability to control the width of the stitch by pulling strands out of the floss, and it's a very durable fiber, not prone to breaking. I work with six-strand embroidery floss and perle cotton, and I also use waxed thread as a stitching workhorse.

Six-Strand Embroidery Floss

There's probably an aisle in your local craft store lined with bins and bins of six-strand embroidery floss in every color under the sun. This is the most commonly used type of embroidery thread because the strands can be separated to create a narrower stitch.

Perle Cotton

Another popular thread, perle cotton is a great option for when you need a thick, sturdy stitch. Perle cotton is a two-ply, non-divisible twisted cotton thread used in appliqué, needlepoint, cross-stitch, and other forms of needlework. Typically sold in balls or skeins, it is less versatile for creating designs because it can't be separated into strands. However, it's much more durable than six-strand floss.

Waxed Thread

I love working with waxed thread, particularly if I'm stitching for strength and the thread isn't going to show on the finished project. It's often marketed as "artificial sinew," and it's great for beadwork, leatherwork, and general stitching. I love using it to sew and gather felt flower petals. It's very strong and long lasting, and it can easily be separated into multiple strands for fine work. I typically use waxed thread in felt and oilcloth flowers.

Baker's Twine

Have you ever thought about stitching with baker's twine? You know, the twirly, multicolored string that's so trendy in crafting, traditionally used by bakers to wrap paper around loaves of bread? It comes in very large spools, and it couldn't be easier to snip off a length to quickly gather some petals or create a decorative stitch around the outside of a leaf.

Floral Tape

Let me tell you a little bit about using floral tape because it can be trickly if you've never used it before. Floral tape is a roll of paper tape that becomes sticky on both sides when you stretch it. I suggest working with small pieces of tape no longer than 5 inches (12.7 cm), and you must continually stretch the tape gently without breaking it to release the gummy stickiness that makes it stick to itself.

Like most crafty skills, you'll continue to improve the more you experiment with it to figure out the right amount of tension you'll need to secure your petals and stems. Try practicing by wrapping it around a pencil. When you do use it for your flower projects, if any of your petals are irregularly shaped, start with the smaller petals in the center and save the larger ones for the outside.

Fabric Stiffener

Sometimes you'll want the fabric in your flowers to have a little added stability without bulking up the fabric's thickness. This is where fabric stiffener comes in: it's a water-based solution that, when it dries, gives your fabric some structure. You'll saturate your fabric with the solution, squeeze out the excess, and then allow the fabric to dry flat or formed to a shaped object.

►►► LEAVES

Whether you want to cut and stitch your own little leaves or bedeck your flowers with millinery findings, you'll have unlimited options when it comes to greening up your pretty fabric blossoms. Here are a couple DIY techniques I like to use.

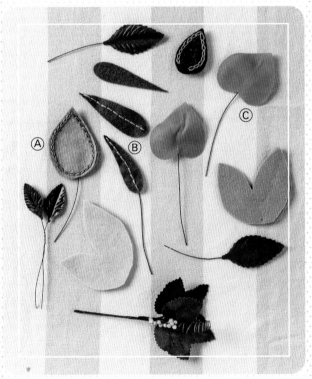

Ⓐ A teardrop-shaped leaf embroidered with a chain-stitch outline

Ⓑ A long, grassy leaf with a straight stitch embroidered down the center, stemmed on a wire

Ⓒ A heart-shaped leaf stemmed on a fabric-covered wire

Tools

Besides buttons and fabric, I keep a fair amount of hardware in my studio for finishing projects, stemming flowers, and making more magic happen! Here are a few other things you'll need to finish the flowers in this book.

Decorative Fabric Shears

I encourage you to keep an eye out for deals on decorative fabric shears. Cutting the edge of a petal with pinking shears, scallop-edged shears, or even wavy-edged shears can change the look and feel of your entire project. I think that the unexpected edges always add an expensive-looking, customized touch.

Needles

Using the right needle for the project makes stitching so much easier. When choosing a needle size, it's best to consider the type of fabric you'll be using. In general, the lighter your fabric, the thinner the needle you'll want to use with it. Hand-sewing needles will work well for lighter fabrics. I recommend using crewel needles for most of the projects in this book because they are designed for use with thicker threads like embroidery floss and perle cotton thread.

Binder Clips

Sometimes you'll want to hold layers of fabric together when you're cutting fringe or petals, or when you're stitching layers of fabric together. I've found that using your everyday office-type binder clips is the perfect fit for clamping fabric together without creasing or tearing it.

Wire Cutters

Each stemmed project calls for floral wire to work as a stem to support the beautiful blossom you've created, and you'll need some heavy-duty snippers depending on the gauge of the wire you use. For thinner wire, you can just use a beat-up pair of scissors, but for the thicker stuff—think 18-gauge and below—you'll want to pick up a pair of wire cutters from a local hobby store.

Millinery Supplies and Stamens

Millinery flowers, leaves, and berries are little wired stems usually made of velvet, silk, paper, or plaster. Realistic stamens, whimsical fruits, or bold blooms were all originally created to adorn hats (necessary, of course, for every well-dressed individual back in the day), but today they're commonly used for a wide variety of projects and crafts. Millinery stems can be found in most craft and hobby stores, but in my opinion the best ones are vintage! Search flea markets, antique stores, eBay and Etsy for these ribbon and fabric treasures.

Templates

Some of the flowers in this book are made with multiples of the same shape, so I've included templates for various petals, leaves, and other little details to make the cutting process a breeze. You'll find the templates in the back of the book printed at their actual size: you only need to photocopy or trace them onto paper, cut them out, and then trace around them onto your fabric. I use tailor's chalk to trace or transfer template shapes, but you could also use a light pencil or another temporary marker of your choice.

▶▶ STAMENS

Adding stamens to the centers of your flowers is another fun way to provide a dimension of personality and individuality. I love to seek out old stamens in vintage stores, and I always keep an eye out for deals online, but it's just as easy to make your own. Here are six quick techniques that can fill out the centers of all the pretty flowers soon to be spread across your worktable. All of these projects can be put together in a matter of minutes with fabric, wire scraps, fabric-covered floral wire, and floral tape: It's a great way to use the pretty little extras you would normally discard after a project!

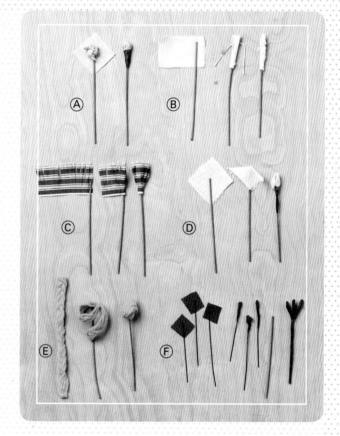

- (A) Place a few fabric scraps in the center of a 1-inch (2.5 cm) square of fabric. Wrap the corners around the scraps and attach to a length of fabric-covered floral wire with floral tape.

- (B) Wrap a length of floral wire with a strip of white chiffon, tying off the top with white thread.

- (C) Fringe a 3-inch (7.6 cm) strip of cotton shirting. Wrap it around a floral wire and secure with floral tape.

- (D) Fold a square of silk or cotton into a triangle, wrap the outer points around a length of fabric-covered floral wire, and fasten with floral tape.

- (E) Braid three ⅛-inch (3 mm) strips of yellow felt. Wrap the braided felt around a length of fabric-covered floral wire. Secure with glue and wrap up to the base with floral tape.

- (F) Wrap three 1-inch (2.5 cm) squares of cotton lawn fabric over the tips of three 2-inch (5.1 cm) pieces of fabric-covered floral wire and secure by wrapping with floral tape. Attach each small stamen to another length of fabric-covered floral wire, staggering them and wrapping up to the base with floral tape.

Running Stitch

Make this stitch by weaving the needle through the fabric at evenly spaced intervals. Lots of straight stitches in a row are called running stitches.

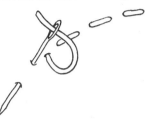

Lazy Daisy

Make a small loop and then anchor it with a single stitch at the top for a decorative stitch that resembles a flower petal.

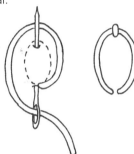

Backstitch

This simple stitch creates a solid line, so it's great for outlining shapes or creating text. You'll stitch backward, inserting your needle at the end of the previous stitch.

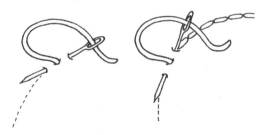

Chain Stitch

This pretty stitch is really a chain of small loops linked together, and it makes a lovely outline or border. To join a circle of chain stitches, stop one stitch short of your first stitch, and slide your needle under the origin of the first stitch, looping back to the origin of your final stitch.

French Knot

This elegant little knot adds interest and texture when embroidering or embellishing. Pull your needle up through the fabric, wrap your floss around the length of the needle, and reinsert the needle just next to where it started. Pull the floss tight and close to the fabric as you pull the needle back through.

Basic
ROSE

Here we have the elegant and dependable rose. Try my simple take on this popular flower that looks as fantastic on its own in your favorite vintage vase as it does arranged in a bouquet. It also lends itself well to the Crowning Glory Headband (see page 93)!

To make one flower:

1 strip of cotton measuring 45 x 3 inches (114.3 x 7.6 cm)

2-inch (5.1 cm) square of cotton (of the same fabric used above, or a matching fabric)

1 fabric-covered floral wire measuring 4 inches (10.2 cm)

Floral tape

Fray Check

Wire cutters

Template (page 125)

make

1 Cut the cotton strip into 18 rectangular pieces, each measuring 2½ x 3 inches (5.7 x 7.6 cm). It helps me to fold the strip in half and mark every 2½ inches (5.7 cm), then cut through both layers of fabric.

2 Using the template as a guide, cut a petal out of each fabric rectangle.

3 Carefully outline the edge of each petal with Fray Check, and allow each petal to dry. This will keep the rose looking delicate and give it a little bit of durability as well.

assemble

Final measurements: Approx 4 inches (10.2 cm) wide

4 Next, make the flower center using the 2-inch (5.1 cm) cotton square. Fold the square of fabric into a triangle, and wrap the outer points around the floral wire. Fasten the fabric to the wire with floral tape.

5 Now, begin adding petals around the flower center. Add the first one by rolling the base of one petal up and holding it between two fingers. Position it next to the flower center and use a small piece of floral tape to wrap them together.

6 Add the next petal by holding the base of the petal to the flower center and securing it with a piece of floral tape. Continue adding petals this way, working around the center of the flower.

FELT
Marigold

This sturdy staple is so brightly colored and downy, it's one of the prettiest blooms in the garden. The fluffy felt version is almost as cheerful as the real thing!

To make one flower:

1 strip of yellow felt measuring
18 x 1½ inches (45.7 x 3.8 cm)

1 circle of yellow felt measuring
1 inch (2.5 cm) in diameter

Perle cotton embroidery thread

1 piece of 9-inch (22.9 cm)
long floral wire

1 button with two buttonholes,
1 inch (2.5 cm) in diameter

Floral tape

Crewel needle

Hot glue gun

Wire cutters

Template (page 126)

1 Cut every 1 inch (2.5 cm)
along the length of the felt
strip to get 18 small rectangles
of felt. Trace the marigold petal
template onto each petal and
carefully cut them out just
inside the traced line.

2 Thread your needle with an
18-inch (45.7 cm) length of
thread. To begin stitching the
petals to the circle base, fold
the edges into the center of
the first petal, then stitch it

to the outer rim of the circle. This will take a few tries to master because the petals are so small, but once you get the hang of it, it will go pretty quickly. Stitch each petal around the diameter of the circle, taking care to bunch them closely together and not leave any spaces.

3 Continue layering petals inside the outer layer. As you fill in the center of the circle base, the bottom edges of the innermost petals will pucker slightly, forming the center of the flower.

4 Fold the piece of floral wire in half and thread the ends of the wire through the buttonholes. Twist the ends of the wires together loosely.

5 Hot glue the base of the marigold to the button on the stem. Finish the flower by wrapping the stem with floral tape.

assemble

Final measurements: 2¾ inches (7 cm) wide

FELTED BALL
Stamens

Turning wool from soft, "cotton-candy-esque" wisps into dense little felt balls is so satisfying. Made tiny, these are the perfect dainty stamens for flowers like roses and poppies. Or create extra-large versions and make a bold statement by arranging them in a graphic vase.

To make one felted ball:

Wool roving

Dish soap (any kind will work)

1 bowl of very hot water

1 bowl of very cold water

1 piece of 26-gauge covered floral wire measuring 9 inches (22.9 cm)

Hot glue gun

Wire cutters

make

1 Tear off a small piece of wool roving. You want a piece that's about 2 inches (5.1 cm) in diameter. It will get much smaller as you work it into a ball.

2 Put a tiny dab of soap in your hands and lightly roll the roving between your palms as if you were shaping a ball of clay. Just form it into a loose, airy ball at first.

3 Dip the wool ball into a bowl of hot water just enough to get it damp, and continue to roll the wool in your hands.

4 As the ball continues to take shape, dip it in your bowl of very cold water to "shock" the fibers.

5 Keep dipping the ball between the hot and cold water as you roll it, rinsing out the soap and felting the wool in the process.

assemble

Final measurements: Approx 1 inch (2.5 cm) wide

6 When the felted wool ball becomes very small and dense, set it on a towel to dry.

7 When the felt sphere dries fully, put a tiny dab of hot glue on the end of the floral wire and wiggle it into the center of the ball. Push the wire through the felted ball until it is about halfway through.

8 Trim the wire to the appropriate length for your flower project.

FELT POM Flower

You'd never be able to tell from the gorgeous results, but these flowers are one of the quickest crafts; you can't ask for more than nearly instant gratification. I love them as pins, mixed into bouquets, or gathered in groups to add instead of bows to my favorite friends' birthday presents. Play around with the width and length of your felt strips and depth and breadth of your snips to switch up the outcome of these playful poms.

gather

To make one flower:

1 strip of felt measuring 30 x 2 inches (76.2 x 5.1 cm)

4 pieces of green felt measuring 2 x 3 inches (5.1 x 7.6 cm)

Green embroidery thread

1 10-inch (25.4 cm) piece of covered floral wire

1 button with large buttonholes, 2 inches (5.1 cm) in diameter

Binder clips

Pinking shears

Hot glue gun

Crewel needle

Template (page 125)

make

1 Fold the large strip of felt in half twice and clip the bottom edge with binder clips to keep the layers together.

2 Trim along one long edge of the felt strip with pinking shears. Use sharp scissors to snip between each zigzag, fringing the fabric through each layer. Snip very close to the base of the strip without cutting all the way through.

assemble

Final measurements: Approx 5 inches (12.7 cm) wide

3 Unfold the fabric and, starting at one end, roll the fringed felt into a coil, gluing the base of the strip underneath the flower to secure it as the flower begins to take shape.

4 Cut two of each leaf shape out of your green felt using the template.

5 Thread the needle with 24 inches (61 cm) of green thread. Layer each matching leaf shape together and backstitch around the outside edges to connect them. If you need a refresher on the backstitch or you want to learn how to do it for the first time, refer the Embriodery Stitch Chart on page 11. Of course, you can also use a different stitch!

6 Glue the leaves to the underside of the flower.

7 Thread the piece of floral wire through the buttonholes of your button, leaving a 1-inch (2.5 cm) tail. Twist the 1-inch (2.5 cm) tail under the button and around the wire, securing it. Glue the button to the underside of the pom flower.

These show-stopping blooms look great in any color. I like to use a bold-colored felt and group mine with other bright flowers, such as a felt posy and cotton lawn rose.

Cotton Pom
BOUQUET

This project is the perfect combination of happy and pretty. The traditionally fancy hand bouquet combines with undeniably whimsical pompoms to make a blissful little bundle you'll be happy to carry and display in your home.

To make 16 flowers:

8 strips of cotton canvas each measuring 2 x 15 inches (5.1 x 38.1 cm)

8 strips of cotton lawn or shirting each measuring 2 x 19 inches (5.1 x 48.3 cm)

16 pieces of green felt each measuring 1½ x 2 inches (3.8 x 5.1 cm)

48 pretty buttons of varying widths and colors

16 boring buttons (for underneath the flower where you won't see them)

8 small white buttons

16 pieces of 20-gauge floral wire measuring 18 inches (45.7 cm) long

Roll of floral tape

2 yards (1.83 m) of 1-inch (2.5 cm) wide satin ribbon

Decorative straight pin

Binder clips

Hot glue gun

Wire cutters

Template (page 126)

1 Fold one of the strips of cotton canvas in half twice, then clip the bottom edge with binder clips to keep it from moving. Fringe the open edge with sharp scissors, taking care not to snip all the way through the fabric to break the strip. Then, you'll be able to unclip the edge and unfold a beautifully fringed strip of canvas.

2 Starting at one end, roll the fringed canvas into a coil. Use a dab of hot glue to secure the end of the strip to the coiled flower. Fuss with the fringe a bit to help the petals of the flower take shape.

3 Use the leaf template to cut a leaf out of one of the pieces of green felt. Snip a small ¼-inch (6 mm) slit in the base of the leaf, as shown.

4 Fold one of the floral wires in half and thread three buttons from your selection of 48 of varying widths and colors onto the wire. Twist the wire a few times right underneath the buttons to secure them at the top, then add three more of these buttons to the wire.

5 Next, thread the pom flower onto the wire by carefully pushing the ends through the center of the coiled flower. Take care not to unravel the flower in the process. Then slide the green felt leaf onto the wire from underneath the flower.

6 Slide one of your boring buttons onto the wire from underneath the flower. This gives the stem some stability so the pom and leaf don't slide down the stem, and you can use any old boring button, because it won't be seen!

7 Holding the pom, twist the two floral wires together to secure the entire shebang.

8 Repeat steps 1 through 7 for the rest of the canvas cotton strips to create seven more flowers for your bouquet.

9 Next, we're going to mix things up and create a slightly different kind of flower to mix into the cotton pom bouquet. Repeat steps 1 through 3 for the cotton lawn strips, fringing and flowering each one and cutting out the leaves.

10 To stem the cotton lawn poms, fold a floral wire in half and slide one small white button on, sliding it all the way up to the top of the bent wire. Then carefully add the cotton lawn pom flower and the leaf.

11 Slide one of your boring buttons up from underneath the flower to hold the whole thing together, then twist the wires together to secure it.

12 Repeat steps 9 through 11 for the other seven strips of cotton lawn.

13 Choose three of your favorites to be positioned in the center of the bouquet. Hold the wire stems of those three flowers and securely wrap them halfway up the stems from the bottom with floral tape, binding them all together.

14 Continue adding and taping each of your pom flowers, both canvas and cotton lawn, one by one, working around the center three flowers you taped and spacing them evenly around the bouquet. When you have them arranged like you want them, tape all of the flowers together halfway up the stems from the bottom, just as you did with the center three.

15 Next, grab your ribbon and glue the end of it about 1 inch (2.5 cm) from the bottom of the stems to anchor it as you start wrapping.

Final measurements: Bouquet, approx 6 inches (15.2 cm) in diameter

16 Put another dab of glue on the end of the stems and pull the ribbon tightly over the end to cover it. Allow the glue to dry so the end stays covered. Continue to wrap the ribbon around the length of the stem, going up, down, and back up again to cover all the floral tape.

17 When you're finished covering the stems, secure the ribbon at the top of the bouquet handle with a dab of glue. Finish it off with a straight pin to keep the ribbon held in tightly and add a polished touch to the bouquet handle.

Felt
POSY

Felt posies are high-impact flowers that are quick and easy to make—perfect for big volume projects. A full tabletop of these beauties can be made in an afternoon, and they combine well with Embroidered Circle Flowers (see page 44) to create giant, bold bouquets.

To make one flower:

1 strip of wool felt measuring 10 x 2 inches (25.4 x 5.1 cm)

1 strip of wool felt measuring 10 x 1.5 inches (25.4 x 3.8 cm)

Waxed thread

1 piece of 18-gauge floral wire measuring 18 inches (45.7 cm)

2 pretty buttons

1 boring button

Crewel needle

Wire cutters

Templates (page 126)

make

1 Cut each strip of felt into ten 1-inch (2.5 cm) pieces to create 20 small felt rectangles.

2 Use the large and small posy petal templates to cut each rectangle into a petal. Sort the petals according to size.

3 Thread your needle with an 18-inch (45.7 cm) length of waxed thread. Sew a loose running stitch along the base of each one of your large petals.

4 Gather the petals on the thread and tie the ends together with a square knot. Trim the threads to about ½ inch (1.3 cm).

5 Repeat steps 3 and 4 with the stack of smaller petals, gathering them and tying the ends of the thread in a knot to secure the flower.

assemble

Final measurements: Approx 3½ inches (8.9 cm) wide

6 With the larger petals as the base, layer the two flowers on top of each other.

7 Fold the floral wire in half and thread the pretty buttons onto the wire. Then thread the two flowers onto the wire.

8 Slide the boring button onto the wire from underneath the flower. This gives the stem some stability so the posy doesn't slide down the stem.

9 Holding the flower, twist the two green wires together to secure it.

CALLA LILY
Bouquet

These classic flowers would make a lovely bouquet in the favorite colors of a friend who is getting married, and the no-sew technique also makes it an easy project to do with kids. Try using buttons in a variety of sizes and colors or vary the size of the flowers for a totally different look.

To make one flower:

1 felt square measuring 3 x 3 inches (7.6 x 7.6 cm)

1 length of 18-guage floral wire measuring 18 inches (45.7 cm)

10 small buttons

1 slightly larger button, about ½ inch (1.3 cm) in size

Fabric glue

Wire cutters

Template (page 124)

make

1 Using the template, cut the petal shape out of the felt.

2 Next, let's do a little folding. Arrange the calla lily shape in front of you with the point facing away from you. Fold the sides of the flower toward the center and secure with fabric glue. This is the basic calla lily shape.

3 To add a stem, fold the piece of floral wire in half. Slide six small buttons onto the wire, threading each end of the wire through the buttonholes so they slide all the way to the top. Then, twist the wires together and add four more buttons.

4 Push the wire down through the center of the felt calla lily and slide the flower up the wire to meet the button stack. The buttons should stick out of the top of the flower like a stamen.

assemble

Final measurements: Each lily, approx 2 inches (5.1 cm) tall

5 Slide the larger button onto the wire to sit underneath the flower and stabilize the stem.

6 Twist the remaining ends of the wire together. If you'd like, wrap the stem with floral tape.

7 Repeat to make as many flowers as desired.

Velvet SUCCULENT

Succulents are unconventionally beautiful, and when they're made from rich velvet, you have something really special. Use them in a brooch or hair clip to show off your nontraditional style, or make a variety and show them off in a Succulent Wreath (see page 118).

(see page 118)

gather

To make one flower:

1 piece of light green velvet measuring 9 x 6¼ inches (22.9 x 15.9 cm)

Purple or magenta permanent marker (optional)

1 circle of green felt measuring 2 inches (5.1 cm) in diameter

Fabric glue

Embroidery floss

Crewel needle

Hot glue gun

make

1 Cut your fabric into five strips: two 9 x 1½ inches (22.9 x 3.8 cm); one 9 x 1¼ inches (22.9 x 3.2 cm); and two 9 x 1 inches (22.9 x 2.5 cm).

2 Set aside one of the 1-inch (2.5 cm) strips and save it for the center of the flower. Snip each velvet strip into nine pieces, each of them 1 inch (2.5 cm) wide.

3 Cut each of the small pieces of velvet into a simple petal shape with a pointed top and wider bottom (almost like a curly bracket on your keyboard).

assemble

Final measurements: Approx 3¾ inches (9.5 cm) wide

4   Add some interest to the petals by coloring the edges of the velvet with permanent marker, if desired.

5   Fold the bottom corners into the center of each petal and use a dab of fabric glue to secure. Make sure that the majority of what is showing on your petal is the fluffy side of the velvet, not the smooth side.

6   Starting with the larger ones, stitch each petal around the outside of the felt circle with the embroidery floss, taking care to bunch them closely together and not leave any spaces.

7   After you finish the first layer of petals, continue with the medium-size petals, layering them over the outside circle of petals. Stitch the end of each one to the felt. Repeat with six of the smallest leaves.

8   After you make three layers of petals, add three more small petals to the center of the flower with glue. Coil the 1-inch (2.5 cm) strip of fabric and glue it to the center of the flower.

Bedeck your tresses by turning this beauty into a stunning hair clip! Hot glue an alligator clip to the back of the flower. Glue a small felt circle over the inside of the clip and to the back of the flower to add a nice finishing touch.

EMBROIDERED
Daisy

Daisies sure are a happy flower, and this one is as fun to make as it is to admire once it's finished! This is the kind of project that's perfect for packing up and taking on the go. Work on the stitches on the bus or in the waiting room so everyone can admire your handiwork.

To make one flower:
4 white felt squares each measuring
4 inches (10.2 cm)

1 circle of yellow felt measuring
1 inch (2.5 cm)

1 strip of green felt measuring
½ x 2 inches (1.3 x 5.1 cm)

Embroidery floss

Fabric-covered floral wire

Floral tape

Crewel needle

Hot glue gun

Wire cutters

Template (page 125)

1 Using the daisy template, cut a flower out of each square of white felt.

2 Thread the needle with 24 inches (61 cm) of embroidery floss. Referring to the Stitch Chart on page 11, do two lazy daisy stitches on each petal radiating from the center of one of the white flowers. Repeat for a second flower so you have two stitched daisies total.

3 Layer one of the stitched flowers on top of a blank white flower. Stitch the two layers together with a simple backstitch around the outline of the flower. (If you need a refresher on the backstitch, or are trying it for the first time, refer to the Stitch Chart on page 11.) Repeat this step for the second flower, stitching both layers together around the outline.

4 Thread your needle and stitch a running stitch around the edge of the yellow felt circle. Wad up a few of your white felt scraps from cutting out the flowers in step 1 and use them to stuff the yellow felt circle. Pull the thread tight, cinching the circle and knotting it closed. Attach the flower center to the stem with floral tape.

5 Now, return to the two flower cutouts you created and stitched. Snip a small slit in the center of each flower and thread the two flowers onto the stem up to the flower center. Fuss with the two flowers a bit so the petals of the bottom flower peek out between the petals of the top flower.

assemble

Final measurements: Each daisy, 3½ inches (8.9 cm) wide

6 Use glue to secure one end of the green felt strip to the stem, right underneath the two daisies. Wrap the piece of felt in a coil around the base of the flower to keep it from sliding down the stem, and glue the other end of the wrap in place as you finish.

Prom
NOSEGAY

One of the best parts of making your own accessories—or crafting in general—is the opportunity for self expression. When you're making something yourself, you don't have to be the same as everyone else. For my senior prom, I didn't want a traditional corsage, so I made myself a nosegay (a tiny, more casual bouquet) to carry in with me. Felt nosegays are especially great since they last forever, a perfect little reminder of a special occasion.

> *gather*

To make 5 flowers:

5 strips of wool felt measuring
20 x 3 inches (50.8 x 7.6 cm)

5 strips of wool felt measuring
20 x 2 inches (50.8 x 5.1 cm)

Waxed thread

5 lengths of 20-gauge floral wire

15-20 of your favorite beautiful
buttons

5 boring buttons

Floral tape

Yarn in your favorite color

1 decorative straight pin

Hand-sewing needle

Hot glue gun

Wire cutters

Templates

> *make*

1 Cut each strip of felt into
ten 2-inch (5.1 cm) pieces to
create ten felt rectangles per
strip. Each flower will be made
of two layers: a bottom layer
of ten 3-inch (7.6 cm) petals
and a top later of ten 2-inch
(5.1 cm) petals.

2 Use any of the petal
templates to cut each
rectangle into a petal. Feel
free to use a variety of the
templates found in this book,
or maybe improvise on a
few of your own. I used a
combination of the Band
T-Shirt Flower Pin petals (page
124) and the Jersey Posy Pin
petals (page 125): variety is
nice in this project!

> *assemble*

Final measurements: Each flower, approx 4½ inches (11.4 cm) wide;
Nosegay, approx 7 inches (17.8 cm) in diameter

3 Thread a needle with an
18-inch (45.7-cm) length of
waxed thread. Sew a loose
running stitch along the base
of 10 large petals.

4 Gather the petals on the thread
and tie the ends together with
a square knot. Trim the threads
to about ½ inch (1.3 cm).

5 Repeat steps 3 and 4 with
ten of the smaller petals,
gathering them and tying the
ends of the thread in a knot
to secure the flower.

6 With the larger petals as the
base, layer the two flowers
on top of each other.

7 Fold the floral wire in half and thread two, three, or even four beautiful buttons onto the wire. Then thread the two flowers onto the wire.

8 Slide one boring button onto the wire from underneath the flower. This gives the stem some stability so the flower doesn't slide down the stem.

9 Holding the flower, twist the two green wires together to secure it.

10 Repeat steps 3 through 9 with the rest of the felt petals to create four more flowers.

11 After all of your flowers are stitched and stemmed, choose your favorite bloom to be positioned in the center of the bouquet. Add each additional flower by securely wrapping the stems together with floral tape, binding them all together.

12 When all of the flowers are taped together, glue the end of your yarn about 1 inch (2.5 cm) from the bottom of the stems. This will be your anchor as you start wrapping the yarn around the stem.

13 Put a dab of glue on the end of the stem and wrap the yarn to cover it. Continue to wrap the yarn around the length of the stem, going up and down and then back up again to cover all of the floral tape completely.

14 When you're finished covering the stem with yarn, secure it at the top of the bouquet handle with a dab of glue. Finish it off with a straight pin to keep the yarn tightly in place and disguise the glue spot.

Felted THISTLES

I love creating these short, sweet little thistles and arranging them in a petite vase. Make as many as you like for anything from a cheerful minimal bloom to a lush, bold bouquet of beautiful buds. Experiment with the stem length and flower size to arrange them with other types of flowers.

To make one flower:

1 piece of green wool felt measuring 5 x 1 inches (12.7 x 2.5 cm)

Wooden skewer (like the ones you use for barbecuing)

Light purple wool roving

Dish soap

Bowl of very hot water

Bowl of very cold water

Pinking shears

Wire cutters

Hot glue gun

make

1 Trim one side of the 1-inch (2.5 cm) strip of green felt with pinking shears.

2 Using sharp scissors, fringe 2 inches (5.1 cm) of the felt strip by snipping into each "valley" of the pinked edge of the felt.

3 Lay the strip of felt flat on the table and, starting from the unfringed end of the strip, use your pinking shears to cut toward the fringing, cutting into the fabric ¼ inch (6 mm) in from the fringed side. Stop trimming once you reach the fringe. You'll be left with a narrow strip of pinked felt with 2 inches (5.1 cm) of long pinked fringe.

assemble

Final measurements: Blooms, approx 1 inch (2.5 cm) wide

4 Use the wire cutters to snip a skewer to 6 inches (15.2 cm) long.

5 Tear a piece from your purple wool roving. You want enough to fit in your hand, roughly the size of a deck of cards.

6 Put a dab of soap in your hands and lightly handle the roving to get it just a little soapy. Gently form the roving into an airy ball shape and roll it in your hands a bit to get the soap on the wool.

7 Dip the wool ball into your bowl of hot water just enough to get it damp, and continue to roll the wool in your hands to form a ball. As it takes shape, dip the ball into the container of cold water to "shock" the fibers; continue to shape the wool in your hands.

8 Keep alternating between hot and cold water as you roll the ball until it is very dense and the soap has been rinsed out. Set the ball on a towel to dry.

9 Wiggle the skewer into the base of your wool felt ball until it feels like it's about halfway into the ball. Secure it with a dab of glue at the base of the stem. Be neat about it, but don't worry about it showing, because it will be covered up by the thistle leaves.

10 Glue the fringed end of the green leaf strip to the stem about ¾ inch (1.9 cm) down from the base of the flower and wind the strip around and down the skewer, securing the end with a dab of glue.

11 Wind the leaf strip around the stem, very slowly working away from the flower base. The fringed part of the leaf will stick out around the bottom of the flower.

Silk
POPPIES

Working with raw silk is fun because it's simple to stitch through and easy to dye. The black centers of these flowers and the rich red petals make these beautiful blooms perfect for pinning in your hair or arranging on the bedside table in your boudoir!

To make one flower:

1 strip of raw silk measuring
15 x 3 inches (38.1 x 7.6 cm)

Cotton ball

1 square of black felt measuring
2 inches (5.1 cm)

Floral tape

2 pieces of fabric-covered floral wire,
each measuring 9 inches (22.9 cm)

Red-colored fabric dye

Bowl of cool water

Wire cutters

Template (page 125)

make

1 Cut the strip of raw silk into six 2½-inch (6.4 cm) pieces. Use the template to cut a petal out of each piece of silk.

2 Next, make the flower center. Pull the cotton ball in half and place one half in the center of the black felt square. Wrap the corners of the square around the cotton ball and twist it around the top of one 9-inch (22.9 cm) wire, like the wrapper on a lollipop. Attach the black flower center to the wire stem with floral tape.

3 Begin attaching the poppy petals. Hold each petal against the center of the flower and fasten it with a small piece of floral tape. Continue adding the rest of the petals—six in total—clockwise around the flower center.

assemble

Final measurements: Each poppy, approx 2½ inches (6.4 cm) tall

4 Attach the flower to the second stem with floral tape. For a nice, uniform look, wrap the entire stem up and down a few times with floral tape.

5 Finally, holding the flower by the stem, dip the petals in the red fabric dye. You can watch the raw silk absorb all of the dye, and twist the flower around a bit to make sure the petals are evenly dyed.

6 Give the petals a quick rinse, dunking them in a bowl of cool water, and allow them to dry hanging upside down. The fabric dye will stiffen the petals a bit too, and as they dry they will take on a beautiful, natural shape.

Embroidered CIRCLE FLOWERS

This is a way to use up scraps of felt to make a nice filler flower for a bouquet or arrangement. Try using decorative scissors to cut out the felt circles for a different look.

To make one flower:
3 or 4 square scraps of felt

Embroidery floss

16 inches (40.6 cm) of green floral wire per flower

A pile of buttons, some boring, some decorative

Crewel needle

Wire cutters

make

1 Cut circles out of your square felt scraps and lay them out on your workspace, layering them in different ways until you figure out how you want each flower to look.

2 Embroider your favorite designs or stitches around the edges of the felt circles to secure each layer to the one beneath it.

3 Fold the green floral wire in half and pick a decorative button or two to become the center of your flower. Slide the button(s) onto the green wire through two of the buttonholes (or through the shank, if you're using a shank button).

assemble

Final measurements: Each flower, 2 to 2½ inches (5.1 to 6.4 cm) wide

4 Push the ends of the wire through the center of the embroidered felt circles and slide them to the top of the wire, snug against the button.

5 Slide one of the more boring buttons onto the wire from underneath the felt circle to give the stem some stability.

6 Twist the remaining floral wire together to finish the stem.

When a bride asked me a few years ago to make her a fabric hydrangea bouquet, I was stumped. I loved the real flowers, but I wasn't sure how to capture the fluffy blossom clusters in fabric. I chose raw silk because it has the same delicacy as the original petals, and the results are SO pretty.

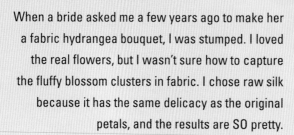

Silk
HYDRANGEAS

To make one flower:

1 strip of raw silk measuring 8 x 1 inches (20.3 x 2.5 cm)

Waxed thread

Violet-colored fabric dye

1 length of 9-inch (22.9 cm) floral wire

1 pearl bead

Crewel needle

Hot glue gun

Wire cutters

Template (page 126)

make

1 Cut the strip of raw silk into eight 1-inch (2.5 cm) pieces.

2 Use the small hydrangea petal template to cut a petal out of each piece of silk.

3 Thread your needle with a 10-inch (25.4 cm) piece of waxed thread.

4 Sew a loose running stitch along the base of each hydrangea petal.

5 Gather the petals on the thread and tie the ends together with a square knot. Trim the thread to about ½ inch (1.3 cm).

assemble

Final measurements: Each hydrangea, 1¾ inches (4.4 cm) wide

6 Dye the flower in a small dish of violet-colored fabric dye. After 5 minutes, gently rinse the flower to give the petals a beautiful purple-wash effect. Allow the flower to dry.

7 Put a dab of hot glue on the end of the floral wire and push it through the center of the pearl bead. Then thread the flower onto the wire and let the glue cool against the petals, securing the flower.

COTTON Carnations

Carnations are my favorite flower. Humble and accessible, they make their greatest impact when grouped together in a large bunch like the ruffles on a petticoat!

gather

To make one flower:

1 strip of cotton lawn measuring 36 x 2 inches (91.4 x 5.1 cm)

1 fabric-covered floral wire measuring 9 inches (22.9 cm)

Floral tape

Pinking shears

Hot glue gun

Wire cutters

make

1 Cut one edge of the cotton lawn strip with pinking shears. As you snip, move your scissors in kind of a wave pattern so the edges of the petals will be somewhat irregular.

2 Snip V shapes into the pinked edge of the fabric to create some individual petals.

3 Coil the cotton lawn strip, using a dab of hot glue here and there to keep the whole thing from unraveling. Pleat the fabric a little bit as you coil it to create a natural petal effect.

assemble

Final measurements: Each carnation, approx 2 inches (5.1 cm) wide

4 Secure the end of the strip with a little hot glue and fluff the petals to shape the carnation flower.

5 While the hot glue is still warm, push the covered floral wire into the base of the flower. Hold it there to secure until the glue is cool.

6 Wrap the base of the flower in floral tape, continuing down the length of the wire stem.

Embroidered Felt
FLOWER BOUQUET

This project can be adapted or changed in so many ways; you can use the same
basic stemming and arranging process to mix in many other types of flowers,
and you can make the bouquet as large or as small as you wish.

To make 16 flowers:

1 yard (91.4 cm) total of wool felt in your favorite colors

1 yard (91.4 cm) of green wool felt

Cotton embroidery floss in your favorite colors

16 awesome buttons

16 boring buttons

16 lengths of 20-gauge floral wire

Floral tape

2 yards (1.8 m) of ivory satin ribbon

4 pearl-head or decorative straight pins

Embroidery needle

⅛-inch (3 mm) hole punch

Fabric glue

Wire cutters

Templates (page 127)

make

1 Use the flower templates to cut out 32 large flower shapes from the felt in your favorite colors.

2 Refer to the templates to cut out 16 medium felt flowers and 16 small ones, also using the felt in your favorite colors.

3 Cut out 32 leaves from the green felt using the leaf template. Pair them up in layers of two and do a simple running stitch around the outside of each leaf to secure the layers together so you end up with a total of 16 stitched leaves.

assemble

Final measurements: Bouquet, approx 6 inches (15.2 cm) in diameter

4 Take some time and arrange the flowers on your workspace the way you would like them to look when they are finished. Start with two large flower bases (I use two instead of one for stability) with a medium layer and a small layer. Think about the color balance and the layering and figure out how you want it all to look.

5 Pick a button to become the center of each flower.

6 Add two matching leaves to each flower to complete the layout.

7 Thread a needle with 24 inches (61 cm) of embroidery floss. Stitch the top three layers of your flower (small, medium, and one of the large bottom layers) together using your favorite embroidery stitches. Refer to the photos or the Stitch Chart on page 11 for ideas.

8 Finish the first flower by adding the second bottom layer to the flower and stitching around the whole piece to add some extra strength and stability.

9 Next, add the stem. Start by folding one of your green floral wires in half. Then, cut a small hole in the center of the flower.

10 Position the center button you have chosen for the flower and push each end of the green wire through the buttonholes into the felt flower.

11 Push the ends of the green wire through the base of one of the stitched leaves and slide it up to the base of the felt flower.

12 Slide one of the boring buttons onto the wire underneath the flower. This gives the stem some stability and keeps the felt flower from sliding down the wire stem.

13 Holding the felt flower, twist the two green wires together to secure the flower.

14 Repeat steps 7 through 13 for the remaining 15 flowers.

15 When all of the flowers are stemmed, choose three of your favorites to become the center of the bouquet.

16 Hold the stems of the three flowers securely and wrap them from the bottom halfway up with floral tape. Continue adding and taping each flower one by one.

17 When all of the flowers are taped together, glue the end of the ribbon about 1 inch (2.5 cm) from the bottom of the stems, with the length of the ribbon trailing straight down like a tail. This will be your anchor as you start wrapping the ribbon around the stem.

18 Tightly pull the ribbon over the bottom of the stems to cover the floral tape. Continue to wrap the ribbon around the length of the stem, going up and down and then back up again.

19 Secure the ribbon by folding it to hide the raw edge and gluing it at the top of the handle. Push the four pins through the ribbon and down into the stem.

Poolside POSY PIN

These giant posy flowers are great for adding some much-needed interest to plain plastic beach totes, the bag you take to the pool, or a cover-up for your swimsuit. You can even attach it to a hair elastic for your post-swim hair! The bright, water-resistant oilcloth won't wilt when splashed, making it perfect for summertime accessories.

To make one flower:

1 oilcloth strip measuring 16 x 1½ inches (40.6 x 3.8 cm)

1 oilcloth strip measuring 16 x 2 inches (40.6 x 5.1 cm)

1 oilcloth strip measuring 16 x 2½ inches (40.6 x 6.4 cm)

Waxed thread

1 big, colorful plastic button

1 brooch pin measuring 1 inch (2.5 cm)

1 super-hardy needle (oilcloth is thick and it can take effort to thread the needle through!)

Templates (page 126)

make

1 Cut each strip into eight 2-inch (5.1 cm) pieces and stack them up according to size, smallest to largest.

2 Use the templates as a guide to cut petals out of each piece of oilcloth. (Be sure to keep the three sizes separate or you might be confused later!)

3 Holding your thumb in the center of each petal, gently pull the fabric outward from the center to create a slight cupped shape.

4 Sew a running stitch through the bottom of each of the smallest petals, gathering each petal along the waxed thread as you go along.

assemble

Final measurements: Approx 4½ inches (11.4 cm) wide

5 When all of the small petals are gathered on the thread, tightly tie the ends of the thread together to keep the petals gathered.

6 Repeat steps 4 and 5 for the medium and large petals.

7 Shape the petals of each flower layer and fluff them out a little bit.

8 Stack the flower layers on top of each other, with the smallest one on top. Stitch through the centers to secure them.

9 Sew the button in the center of the smallest flower. You can also cover a button in leftover oilcloth if you're feeling really crafty.

10 Stitch the pin back to the underside of the flower and head out for some summertime fun!

Soft Pink Rose
BOUTONNIERE

Fabric flowers can be bold, bright fashion statements, but let's be honest: sometimes you just want something soft and pretty! Roses are a floral staple for a reason, with their sweetly complex shape and dreamy connotations. Wear this boutonniere when you want to add romance to a nearly perfect date outfit, or dress up a group of groomsmen on your special day.

To make one flower:

1 strip of cotton measuring 22½ x 3 inches (57.2 x 7.6 cm) with one frayed edge (snip the fabric on the grain and tear it up the length of the yardage)

1 vintage millinery ball stamen

1 8-inch (20.3 cm) piece of 20-gauge floral wire, folded in half

Floral tape

1 length of yarn measuring 10 inches (25.4 cm)

Straight boutonniere pin

Hot glue gun

Template (page 125)

make

1 Cut the fabric into nine pieces measuring 2½ x 3 inches (6.4 x 7.6 cm). It helps me to fold the strip in half and mark every 2½ inches (6.4 cm), then cut through both layers of fabric.

2 Using the template as a guide, cut a petal out of each fabric rectangle. Position the template so the top edge of the petal is aligned with the frayed edge of the fabric.

3 Start by making the flower center. Roll up the base of one petal and hold it between two fingers. Position it next to the vintage ball stamen and the folded floral wire, and use a small piece of floral tape to wrap them together. This is going to be the anchor for attaching the rest of the petals.

assemble

Final measurements: Approx 3¾ inches (9.5 cm) wide

4   Continue adding petals and securing them with small pieces of floral tape. I like to grip the base of the flower and hold the tape in place with my thumb while I add petals two or three at a time.

5   As you add more and more petals, the stamen wire will become pretty thick with floral tape. Try to concentrate the bulk of the tape around the base of the petals, and fold the stamen wire up on the thick base and cover it with floral tape. The wire stamen stem is just for some stability, but as you keep wrapping it'll become increasingly sturdy.

6   Wrap the floral tape base of the flower with yarn and secure it with hot glue.

7   Attach it to your lapel (or the lapel of one of your favorite people) with a boutonniere pin.

Cotton Dahlia
HAIR CLIP

What's not to love about the open exuberance and richness of the dahlia?
Mexico's national flower is the tropical cousin of the friendly daisy and lends
itself perfectly to providing that pop of color you want in your wardrobe.
This dahlia project would be beautiful recreated in bright hues like hot pink,
yellow, and orange, and pinned into loose curls for your next fiesta.

To make one flower:

3 cotton lawn strips measuring
9 x 1½ inches (22.9 x 3.8 cm)

2 cotton lawn strips measuring
9 x 1¼ inches (22.9 x 3.2 cm)

2 cotton lawn strips measuring
9 x 1 inches (22.9 x 2.5 cm)

1 circle of wool felt measuring
2 inches (5.1 cm) in diameter

1 scrap of wool felt (for adhering the
flower to a bobby pin)

Fabric glue

Bobby pins

Templates (page 124)

make

1 Reserve one of the 1-inch (2.5 cm) strips for the flower center. Snip each of the remaining cotton lawn strip into nine pieces, each of them measuring 1 inch (2.5 cm) wide.

2 Trace the cotton dahlia templates onto the stack of cotton pieces, using the larger pieces for the larger petals, and cut out the petals just inside the traced line. Fold the edges of each petal into the center and use a dab of fabric glue to secure. It helps to use a bobby pin to hold each petal closed until the glue dries.

3 Starting with the larger petals, glue each petal around the outside of the felt circle, taking care to bunch them closely together and not leave any spaces. After you finish the first layer of petals, continue with the medium

assemble

Final measurements: 4 inches (10.2 cm) wide

and smaller petals, layering them over the outer circle of larger petals. Glue the base of each one to the felt.

4 After you finish all the layers of petals, fringe the last 1-inch (2.5 cm) strip of fabric and roll it into a coil. Glue the fringed coil to the center of the flower.

5 Glue the wool felt scrap to one side of the bobby pin, and then glue it to the wool felt circle at the back of the flower.

RUFFLED JERSEY
Flower Pin

Jersey is as unfussy and easy to work with as it is to wear. It's stretchy and forgiving to beginning stitchers, and there's no need to finish the edges. This pin will add interest to your favorite comfy tee, or pair it with more formal fabrics like wool or tweed.

To make one flower:

1 strip of jersey measuring 20 x 1½ inches (50.8 x 3.8 cm)

1 strip of jersey measuring 20 x 1 inches (50.8 x 2.5 cm)

1 square of jersey measuring 3 x 3 inches (7.6 x 7.6 cm)

1 square of felt measuring 2 x 2 inches (5.1 x 5.1 cm)

Embroidery floss

1 pin back measuring 1 inch (2.5 cm)

Crewel needle

Fabric glue

make

1 Gather the wider strip of jersey by sewing a loose running stitch along the bottom of the strip. Then, push the fabric along the floss and tie the two ends of floss in a knot to secure. Fuss with the ruffles a bit to even them out.

2 Repeat step 1 with the other strip of jersey.

3 Cut the larger jersey square into a circle, and save the scraps.

4 Sew a running stitch around the outside of the circle you've created and leave the ends of the thread free. Gather the circle to create a small bowl shape.

5 Stuff the inside of the gathered circle with the scraps from cutting out the circle. Cinch the

assemble

Final measurements: 3¼ inches (8.3 cm) wide

ends of the thread together and tie them to secure it. Roll the ball between your hands to shape it.

6 Place the smaller ruffled flower from step 2 on top of the larger one from step 1 and put a few stitches through the middle to secure them to each other.

7 Stitch the jersey ball to the center of the pleated flower.

8 Cut the smaller felt square into a circle and stitch the pin back to it. Glue the felt circle to the back of the flower.

JERSEY
Posy Pin

The simple design of this flower makes it possible to create with any fabric. Posies are a great way to use up scraps, or to incorporate expensive fabric into your wardrobe and décor without a big investment. I really like using jersey for a fluffier, more casual result.

To make one flower:

1 jersey fabric strip measuring
30 x 3 inches (76.2 x 7.6 cm)

1 jersey fabric strip measuring
32 x 2½ inches (81.3 x 6.4 cm)

1 jersey fabric strip measuring
36 x 2 inches (91.4 x 5.1 cm)

Waxed thread

1 brooch pin measuring ¾ inch
(1.9 cm)

Hand-sewing needle

Templates (page 125)

> *assemble*

Final measurements: Approx 4½ inches (11.4 cm) wide

➤ *make* ➤

1 Cut every 2½ inches (6.4 cm) along the widest fabric strip to create 12 large rectangles. Cut every 2 inches (5.1 cm) along the medium strip to create 16 medium rectangles, and every 1½ inches (3.8 cm) along the thinnest fabric strip to create 24 small rectangles. Separate all of the fabric pieces by size.

2 Use the templates as a guide to cut petals out of each piece of jersey in each stack. You will end up with stacks of large, medium, and small petals.

3 Starting with the large petals, hold your thumb in the center of each petal and gently pull the fabric outward from the center to create a slight cupped shape.

4 Sew a running stitch through the bottom of each of the large petals, gathering them along the waxed thread as you go.

5 When all of the large petals are on the thread, tie the ends of the thread to gather all of the petals together.

6 Repeat steps 4 and 5 for the medium and small petals.

7 Shape the petals of each flower as in step 3 and fluff them out a little bit.

8 Stack the flowers on top of each other with the smallest flower on top. Stitch through the centers to secure them.

9 Stitch a pin back to the underside of the flower to complete your posy.

BEE & BLOSSOM
Sweater Clip

A little felt bee buzzes around a sunny felt marigold, making an adorable accessory that keeps your cardigan closed and your friends abuzz about how cute you've been looking lately.

To make one flower and one bee:

1 piece of yellow felt measuring 10 x ½ inches (25.4 x 1.3 cm)

1 yellow felt circle measuring 1 inch (2.5 cm) in diameter

2 squares of yellow felt measuring 1½ inches (3.8 cm)

Small scrap of white felt

White embroidery floss

Black embroidery floss

4 jump rings

1 chain measuring 7 inches (17.8 cm)

1 chain measuring 9 inches (22.9 cm)

2 alligator clips with holes in the base

Needle-nose pliers

Crewel needle

Hot glue gun

Templates (page 124)

make

1 Use the needle-nose pliers to gently open one of the jump rings. Thread a jump ring through each end of the 7-inch (17.8 cm) chain and attach one end to each of the top holes in the alligator clips. Repeat this with the 9-inch (22.9 cm) chain, attaching the ends to the bottom holes in the alligator clips and laying the chain out to make sure it won't get twisted when you wear the finished sweater clips. (You can source chains for the sweater clips from a local craft store, or you can dig into your own jewelry box or surf the vintage shops for antique chains with a little more character.)

assemble

Final measurements: Bee, 1 inch (2.5 cm) wide; Bloom, 1¾ inches (4.4 cm) wide

2 Cut every ½ inch (1.3 cm) along the length of the felt strip to get 20 small squares of felt. Trace the marigold petal template onto each petal and carefully cut them out just inside the traced line.

3 Thread your needle with an 18-inch (45.7 cm) length of white floss (I used red and white floss in the assembly photo). To begin stitching the petals to the 1-inch (2.5 cm) circle base, fold the edges into the center of the first petal, then stitch it to the outer rim of the circle. This will take a few tries to master because the petals are so small, but once you get the hang of it, it will go pretty quickly. Stitch each petal around the diameter of the circle, taking care to bunch them closely together and not leave any spaces.

4 Continue layering petals inside the outer layer. As you fill in the center of the circle base, the bottom edges of the innermost petals will pucker slightly, forming the center of the flower.

5 Next, make the sweet little bee. Trace the bee body template onto the two yellow squares of felt and cut them out just inside the traced line. Embroider the bee stripes with a tight black chain stitch, starting the stripes about one-quarter of the way down the body to leave room for a head. Use French knots to make two little eyes (see the Stitch Chart on page 11).

6 Trace the bee wing template onto your piece of white scrap felt. Cut it out and secure the wings to the back of the bee with a few stitches of white embroidery floss.

7 Use hot glue to secure the marigold and bee to each sweater clip. Attach each side to the collar of your favorite cardigan and let the compliments roll in!

Pleated Felt
HEADBAND

In the Midwest, where I live, a heavy headband like this one is perfect for keeping my ears warm in chilly weather as I dash around town, and keeping my hair cute when it's up in a messy bun. I love making this headband monochromatic, but experimenting with color, or even adding a second flower, would lend an entirely different look to this simple project.

To make one headband and one flower:

1 strip of felt measuring 54 x 3 inches (137.2 x 7.6 cm)

1 strip of felt measuring 36 x 2 inches (91.4 x 5.1 cm)

2 circles of felt each measuring 1 inch (2.5 cm) in diameter

1 felt scrap measuring 3 x ¼ inches (7.6 cm x 6 mm)

1 skein of embroidery floss

Perle cotton thread

1 piece of 2-inch (5.1 cm) wide black ribbed elastic measuring 4 to 6 inches (10.2 to 15.2 cm) long

1 bar pin measuring 1 inch (2.5 cm)

Straight pins

Tailor's chalk

Iron

Crewel needle

Hot glue gun

Template (page 126)

make

1 Create a simple pleat along the length of your larger felt strip by marking every 1 inch (2.5 cm) with tailor's chalk. Every other 1 inch (2.5 cm) along the strip, use the marks as a guideline to fold the felt over itself; pin to secure it. Continue until the entire strip is pleated, then iron the strip to get those pleats firmly in place.

2 Thread your needle with 18 inches (45.7 cm) of embroidery floss and stitch two rows down the center of the strip to secure the pleats. I used a backstitch here, but a chain stitch or a running stitch would work well, too (see the Stitch Chart on page 11 for more on embroidery stitches).

assemble

Final measurements: Flower, 3½ inches (8.9 cm) wide

Just be sure to stitch over the fold of each pleat so that they're completely secure.

3 Hold the headband up to your head to measure how much elastic you need to secure it, and carefully hot glue the elastic to each end on the underside of the headband to close it up.

4 Cut every 1½ inches (3.8 cm) along the 36 x 2-inch (91.4 x 5.1 cm) strip of felt to make a pile of 24 small rectangles. Trace the headband petal template onto the petal pieces and cut each one out just inside the traced line.

5 Thread your needle with 18 inches (45.7 cm) of perle cotton thread. Fold the edges of one petal toward the

center of the petal. Stitch it to the outer edge of one of the small felt circles. Continue clockwise around the edge of the felt circle, folding the petals and stitching them securely to the base. Once you finish the first layer of petals around the perimeter of the circle, continue onto the next layer, stitching each petal to the center of the circle base.

6 Finely fringe the 3 x ¼-inch (7.6 cm x 6 mm) felt scrap and roll it into a coil. Glue it to the center of the flower.

7 Cut two slits 1 inch (2.5 cm) apart in the second felt circle. Open the bar pin and feed it through the two slits so that the back is hidden by the circle. Close the pin and glue the felt circle to the back of the flower.

8 Pin the flower to the headband. Wear it with your favorite pea coat to keep your ears warm and your hair stylish!

RUFFLED FELT
Prize Ribbon

These miniature prize ribbons are reminiscent of the first-place ribbons I fantasized about receiving as a child for my imaginary rabbits or nonexistent champion show horse. Once you learn the process of ruffling a strip of fabric, you'll be able to recreate these ribbons with all kinds of different fabrics and materials. They're great for birthday parties or bridal showers, or just to pin to your bag to show that you're #1 at being you!

▸ *gather* ▸

To make one flower:

1 strip of felt measuring 36 x 1 inches (91.4 x 2.5 cm)

1 felt circle measuring 2 inches (5.1 cm) in diameter

Embroidery floss

A few buttons you can layer in the center of the flower

Your favorite grosgrain ribbon (I like to use one that is 2 inches [5.1 cm] or wider)

1 brooch pin measuring 1 inch (2.5 cm)

Crewel needle

Lighter

Hot glue gun

▸ *make* ▸

1 Thread your needle with some embroidery floss and get ready to ruffle that felt! Pleat the felt by folding up ½ inch (1.3 cm) of felt every ½ inch (1.3 cm) along the strip, hand-stitching down the side of the strip to secure the pleats. I like to use embroidery floss for this because the contrasting colors are so nice to look at— just a small pleasure.

2 As you continue to fold each bit of the felt strip over on itself and hand-sew along the edge, the strip will begin to curl and twist up. That's good!

▸ *assemble* ▸

Final measurements: 3 inches (7.6 cm) wide

3 Coil the pleated felt strip into a circle roughly 3 inches (7.6 cm) in diameter and make a few stitches to secure the ends together.

4 Stitch the buttons to the center of the flower. Ooh la la.

5 Cut a length of grosgrain ribbon measuring 4 inches (10.2 cm) long. I like to snip the end of my ribbon in a V shape and use a lighter to gently singe the edges, protecting the ribbon from fraying. Glue the ribbon to the back of the pleated flower so the tail hangs down below like a prize ribbon.

6 Snip two small slits in the felt circle about 1 inch (2.5 cm) apart. Open the pin back and feed it through the two slits in the circle, so the middle of the bar is hidden. Close the pin and hot glue the circle to the back of the flower.

Layer ribbons underneath the flower for a different look, or try using a variety of buttons for the flower center.

Daisy HAIRPINS

Is there anything in the world more cheerful than a daisy? When this happy little flower is backed with a simple hairpin, it adds a bit of spring to every room you enter. This project comes together quickly and easily using some very basic techniques. Make a bunch of these and pair them with a wraparound braid for a perfect daisy crown.

To make one flower:

3 squares of white muslin each measuring 1½ inches (3.8 cm)

Fabric stiffener

2 yellow buttons

Yellow em broidery floss

Bobby pin

Iron

Crewel needle

Hot glue gun

make

1 Spray the muslin with fabric stiffener and allow it to dry.

2 Fold the muslin as if you were making a paper snowflake: fold the square in half diagonally to make a triangle, then in half again so the pointy corners meet. Fold the pointed corners together again.

3 Iron the triangle thoroughly to make the crisp, pleated petals of the daisy.

4 Cut a deep V into the top of the triangle. Not sure if your folds and cuts are aligned? Test them out on a scrap of fabric or paper first.

5 Unfold the muslin to reveal the star-like shape. Repeat with the other muslin squares.

assemble

Final measurements: Each daisy, approx 1½ inches (3.8 cm) wide

6 Stack the three layers together, fanning out the petals so they all peek through each other.

7 Stack the yellow buttons in the center of this new flower and stitch them in place with yellow embroidery floss.

8 Glue the bobby pin to the back of the daisy.

Cotton Lawn PEONY PIN

They may look delicate, but the lush layers of soft cotton lawn petals are held together securely with waxed thread, one of my favorite supplies of all time. The stamens in the center can be new, vintage, or even handmade, and you could also make this peony out of different fabrics or add leaves.

gather

To make one flower:

1 strip of cotton lawn measuring 36 x 3 inches (91.4 x 7.6 cm)

1 strip of cotton lawn measuring 36 x 2 inches (91.4 x 5.1 cm)

1 strip of cotton lawn measuring 20 x 1½ inches (50.8 x 3.8 cm)

1 circle of wool felt measuring 2 inches (5.1 cm) in diameter

Waxed thread

Fabric dye one shade darker than your fabric

8 small vintage millinery stamens

1 bar pin measuring 1 inch (2.5 cm)

Hand-sewing needle

Small glass bowl of hot water

Hot glue gun

Templates (page 127)

make

1 Cut every 2 inches (5.1 cm) along the 36 x 3-inch (91.4 x 7.6 cm) strip of cotton lawn to create 18 rectangles of fabric. Trace the large petal template onto each piece of fabric, and cut out the pattern just inside the traced line. I like to stack up three or four petals at a time to cut them out all at once.

assemble

Final measurements: Approx 5½ inches (14 cm) wide

2 Cut the 36 x 2 inches (91.4 x 5.1 cm) of cotton lawn fabric the same way, this time snipping every 1 inch (2.5 cm) along the length of the fabric to create 36 medium fabric rectangles. Cut the 20 x 1 inches (50.8 x 2.5 cm) of cotton lawn fabric the same way, snipping every 1 inch (2.5 cm) along the length to create 20 small fabric rectangles. Divide all the fabric into two stacks for the small- and medium-size petal templates. Trace the templates onto each stack and cut them out just inside the traced line. Again, it's a great idea to cut out several petals at once, stacking them up and cutting through all the layers.

3 Thread your needle with an 18-inch (45.7 cm) length of waxed thread. Take your stack of large petals and sew a loose running stitch through

the base of each one. Gather the petals on the thread and tie the ends together with a square knot. Trim the threads to about ½ inch (1.3 cm). Fuss with the petals a bit to get them all facing up and looking the way you want them to. Repeat separately with the medium-size and small petals, gathering them on your thread and tying them off.

4 Fill a small glass bowl about halfway with steaming hot water. Mix in a little bit of fabric dye (a little goes a long way). What you're looking for is to tint your fabric rather than do a really saturated color.

5 Hold the largest flower by the tops of the petals and dip the base of the flower into the fabric dye, saturating the bottom third of the petals. After the flower is saturated, gently rinse the dye out with cool water. (This will wash away most of the dye; you just want a hint of color!) Set the flower upside down on a piece of newspaper to dry. Repeat for the medium and small flowers, dipping their bases into the dye and rinsing gently with cool water. Wait until the flower layers are dry to the touch before continuing. You can speed this process with a hair dryer, if you wish.

6 Layer the flowers on top of each other, with the largest one as the base. Insert the wire ends of the stamens through the centers of each flower layer and bend them underneath the flower. Use a dab of hot glue to secure them underneath the peony.

7 Snip two small slits in the felt circle about 1 inch (2.5 cm) apart. Open the pin back and feed it through the two slits in the circle, so the middle of the bar is hidden. Close the pin and hot glue the circle to the back of the flower.

CARNATION
Lapel Pin

Carnations are the fluffy, affordable underdogs of the chilly supermarket
flower case, and in my years of bouquet making I've fallen in love with
their simple charm. Look closer at these blossoms and you'll see a fan of
feathery petals that is complex and surprisingly pretty. Light, airy colors
make it sweet, but patterned scraps can make this standard flower into
something bold and unexpected.

To make one flower:

1 cotton lawn strip measuring 12 x 3 inches (30.5 x 7.6 cm)

Thread

Fuchsia-colored fabric dye

1 green floral wire measuring 6 inches (15.2 cm)

Floral tape

Straight pin

Hand-sewing needle

Small glass bowl

make

1 Snip the edge of the cotton strip and tear the fabric down the length of the strip to fray the edge.

2 Cut V-shaped notches here and there into the frayed edge of the strip to make subtle carnation petals.

3 Sew a running stitch along the cut edge of the fabric strip, gathering the petals and stitching them into place every 3 to 4 inches (7.6 to 10.2 cm).

assemble

Final measurements: Carnation, approx 2½ inches (6.4 cm) wide

4 Keep gathering your running stitch along the edge of the fabric and coiling the petals into place.

5 When you finish the length of the petal strip, anchor the coiled petals with a few stitches and fluff the petals to shape the carnation flower. Trim any errant strings on the frayed edge.

6 Fill a small bowl with a little bit of fabric dye. Dip the frayed tips of the carnation petals in the dye and set them aside to dry. (You can speed this process with a hair dryer!)

7 Fold the green floral wire in half and gently push the ends through the center of the carnation, taking care not to loosen the petals.

8 Wrap the floral wire in floral tape, starting from the bottom. As you get toward the top of the stem, wrap the base of the carnation in tape to secure it to the stem.

9 Curl up the end of the stem and attach it to your lapel with the straight pin.

This simple bloom looks great as a dainty lapel pin or as boutonnieres for, say, a group of groomsmen. Try wrapping three together for a more dramatic corsage.

FABRIC *Blooms*

Pom FASCINATOR

You can knock out this high-impact hair accessory in less than half an hour, making it a great last-minute gift idea or a show-stopping adornment you can whip up for an unexpected party when your usual baubles lose their appeal.

>> gather

To make one flower:

1 strip of felt measuring 3 yards x 1 inch (2.7 m x 2.5 cm)

1 felt circle measuring 3 inches (7.6 cm) in diameter

1 barrette measuring 2 inches (5.1 cm)

Fabric glue

Hot glue gun

>> make

1 Use sharp scissors to fringe the felt strip, snipping very close to the base of the strip (but not all the way through!) about every ¼ inch (6 mm) along the length of the felt. I find it easier to fold the felt in half and do two layers at once, but even if you aren't comfortable doing that, it won't take you too long.

2 Roll the fringed felt into a coil, gluing the base of the strip underneath the flower with fabric glue to secure it as the flower begins to take shape.

3 Make sure the felt circle is the same diameter as your flower. If it's too big, you can trim it a bit.

>> assemble

Final measurements: 4¾ inches (12 cm) wide

4 Hot glue the felt circle to the underside of the flower and stitch or glue the barrette clip to the base. Wear it on your pretty little head at the most jaunty angle you can muster.

BAND T-SHIRT
Flower Pin

It would be easy to use this T-shirt technique in almost any of the other flower projects to create an entire bouquet of blooms that remind you of your favorite concerts.

To make one flower:

1 favorite old T-shirt you don't mind cutting up

Waxed thread

1 brooch pin measuring ¾ inch (1.9 cm)

Hand-sewing needle

Template (page 124)

make

1 Cut out thirty 2 x 3-inch (5.1 x 7.6 cm) rectangles from the jersey fabric of the T-shirt. Use as much as you can of the main design of the shirt so it will show up on the finished flower.

2 Use the template to cut each rectangle into a petal.

3 Thread your needle with an 18-inch (45.7 cm) length of waxed thread. Sew a loose running stitch along the base of each one of your petals. Gather the petals on the thread and tie the ends together with a square knot. Trim the threads to about ½ inch (1.3 cm). Fuss with the petals a bit to show off the design on the fabric.

4 Cut a 2-inch (5.1 cm) circle out of the T-shirt fabric and sew a loose running stitch around the outside of the circle. Pull the ends of the thread gently to begin to gather the circle into a cup shape.

5 Stuff a few fabric scraps into the center of the gathered circle and cinch the ends of

assemble

Final measurements: Approx 3¾ inches (9.5 cm) wide

the thread to close it up. Tie the ends of the thread in a knot and roll the ball gently in your hands to shape the center of the flower.

6 Stitch the flower center to the middle of the jersey petals

7 Stitch the brooch pin to the back of the flower.

CHERRY BLOSSOM
Lapel Pin

Cherry blossoms have long been a symbol of surprising beauty and ethereal sweetness, and they're a little more unexpected as an accessory than a dahlia or a daisy. Experiment with the scale of your petals and group these flowers in bunches of two or more to mimic the organic shapes of natural sakura blossoms.

To make two flowers:

2 scraps of pale pink cotton lawn measuring 3 x 3 inches (7.6 x 7.6 cm)

2 scraps of green cotton lawn measuring 3 x 3 inches (7.6 x 7.6 cm)

Fabric stiffener

Floral tape

10 small millinery stamens with black heads

2 pieces of 22-gauge green floral wire each measuring 6 inches (15.2 cm)

Straight boutonniere pin

1/16-inch (1.6 mm) hole punch

Hot glue gun

Wire cutters

Templates (page 124)

make

1 Saturate each piece of fabric with fabric stiffener and set them aside to dry. You can speed this process with a hair dryer if you don't want to wait!

2 Trace the cherry blossom petal template onto the pieces of pale pink cotton and the calyx template onto the pieces of green cotton. Cut them out carefully to avoid fraying.

3 Use the hole punch to punch a tiny hole in the center of each flower and calyx.

4 Using floral tape, attach five small millinery stamens to the end of one of the floral wires. Thread the wire through the center of a petal until it reaches the base of the stamens. Then thread the wire through the green calyx, sliding it behind the petal. Add

assemble

Final measurements: Each blossom, approx 2 inches (5.1 cm) wide

a dab of hot glue to the center of the cotton calyx before it reaches the back of the petal, securing both layers to the stem. Repeat with the stamens, second piece of floral wire, and the remaining petal and calyx layers to create two cherry blossom stems.

5 Wrap each individual stem in floral tape up to the cotton calyx. Arrange the two stems together and secure them to each other with a little bit of floral tape. Use the straight pin to attach them to your shirt or the lapel of a jacket.

SUNFLOWER
Pin

Once you get the hang of French knots—the embroidery technique used here to reproduce the seedy sunflower centers—you can use it to add pretty texture to all sorts of craft projects. I love using them here to draw attention to the unique shape of these blooms. They make this felt version just as cheerful and sunshiny as the real thing.

To make one flowers:

8 strips of yellow felt measuring
12 x 1 inches (30.5 x 2.5 cm)

2 squares of brown felt measuring
3 x 3 inches (7.6 x 7.6 cm)

Waxed thread

Brown embroidery floss

1 brooch pin measuring 1 inch (2.5 cm)

Iron

Crewel needle

Pinking shears

Fabric glue

Template (page 126)

make

1 Cut each strip of felt into four 3-inch (7.6 cm) pieces to create a total of 32 felt rectangles.

2 Use the sunflower petal template to cut each rectangle into a petal. Press each one in half lightly with an iron.

3 Using pinking shears, cut one square of brown felt into a circle.

4 Sew a loose running stitch along the bases of 16 petals. Gather the petals on the thread and tie the ends together in a square knot. Stitch one brown felt circle to the back of this first layer of petals.

assemble

Final measurements: Approx 6 inches (15.2 cm) wide

5 Cut the other square of brown felt into a circle.

6 Repeat step 4 with the remaining 16 petals, and stitch the second brown felt circle to the front of these petals with a simple running stitch.

7 Thread your needle with about 12 inches (30.5 cm) of brown floss and add some pretty pollen to the center of the sunflower by stitching French knots through the petals and brown felt circle (see the Stitch Chart on page 11).

8 Using fabric glue, sandwich the two flower layers together.

9 Glue the brooch pin to the back of the sunflower.

CROWNING GLORY
Headband

One of my favorite trends is flower headbands. They're whimsical in a tall, teased-up hairdo, and they can be sweet and demure on a little girl in your life. Once you get the hang of this technique, you can recreate it with any flower type, different colors, and other fabrics for a variety looks.

To make one headband:

7 strips of felt, any color, measuring 12 x 1½ inches (30.5 x 3.8 cm)

2 strips of felt, any color, measuring 12 x 1 inches (30.5 x 2.5 cm)

1 strip of green felt measuring 18 x 2 inches (45.7 x 5.1 cm)

9 or more wire millinery stamens

Headband blank

3 yards (2.7 m) of yarn

Hot glue gun

Templates (pages 126)

> make >

1 This headband features seven large roses and two smaller roses. Make a larger rose by cutting one of the 1½-inch (3.8 cm) strips of felt into 12 pieces measuring 1 x 1½ inches (2.5 x 3.8 cm). Use the templates to cut a petal out of each piece of felt.

2 Start by creating the center of one flower. Draw a bead of hot glue along the base of a petal and wrap it around one or more, if you like, of the wire millinery stamens. Hold it in place for a moment to form it around the stem. This is going to be the anchor as you add the rest of your petals.

3 Add the next petal the same way, on the opposite side of the stamen. Continue adding petals clockwise around the petal base using small dabs of hot glue until you've added all 12 petals to the first flower.

> assemble >

Final measurements: Arc of flowers, approx 8 inches (20.3 cm) long

4 Set the first flower aside, admire it for a moment, and then repeat steps 1 through 3 to create the remaining six flowers from the 1½-inch (3.8 cm) strips.

5 Repeat steps 1 through 3 to create the flowers from the 1-inch (2.5 cm) strips, this time cutting 12 pieces from each strip measuring 1 x 1 inch (2.5 x 2.5 cm). I used both the pointed and flat-bottomed petal templates for these.

6 Wrap the headband blank with yarn. It's simple to say but there are a few ways to do this step. I've found that the easiest way to do it is to cut the yarn in half and wrap the headband in two steps, because working with long lengths of yarn while wrapping can be tricky. Use a small dab of hot glue to secure the beginning of the thread underneath the headband before you start wrapping, and use a tiny dab at the very end as well. Keep the glue under the headband so it won't be seen. It's also possible to cheat and skip this step by using a pre-wrapped headband, of course, but I love the look of the yarn and the way it grips the hair when it's worn. I will also add that wrapping a headband gets easier with practice.

7 Fuss with the flowers a little bit, holding them up to the headband, and decide in which order you'd like to attach them. Once you decide, begin in the middle.

8 Wrap the wire stamen of the first flower around the center of the headband. Take care to tuck the end of the wire underneath the headband. Then, working from the center flower, add each flower the same way, wrapping the wire stamen underneath the headband. Don't worry too much about the wire showing; we'll cover it up in the next step.

9 Cut the green strip of felt into 18 pieces measuring 1 x 2 inches (2.5 x 5.1 cm). Use the leaf template on page 126 to cut a leaf shape out of each piece. Use your judgment (and a dab of hot glue) to secure each leaf to the underside of the headband, covering up all of the stamen wire messiness.

»

Crown yourself with this cheerful floral goodness. Aren't you just the queen of the wildflowers?

EMBROIDERED FELT
Flower Pin

For me, the best part of making these pins is the endless color combinations. I like to cut out enough material to make four or five, then spend time arranging the felt layers to show color in unexpected ways. The extras make great presents, and everybody loves the vintage button detail. One of these embroidered pins will always have a place on my winter pea coat.

> *gather*

To make one flower:

6 squares of wool felt each measuring 3 x 3 inches (7.6 x 7.6 cm)

Cotton embroidery floss in your favorite colors

1 awesome button

1 brooch pin measuring 1 inch (2.5 cm)

Embroidery needle

Templates (page 127)

> *make*

1 Use the flower templates to cut out two large flower shapes, one medium flower shape, and one small flower shape from the squares of wool felt, then use the leaf template to cut two leaves out of felt, too.

2 Thread a needle with 24 inches (61 cm) of embroidery floss in your favorite color. Layer the two leaf shapes together and stitch the outside edges together using a running stitch or your favorite embroidery stitch.

3 Stitch the top three layers of your flower together using your favorite embroidery stitches, leaving the bottom flower layer out. If you need embroidery ideas, see the Stitch Chart on page 11.

4 Sandwich the stitched leaves between the stitched flower and the leftover large flower shape. Secure the whole piece by stitching around the flower edges. The extra flower sewn to the back gives it some strength and stability.

> *assemble*

Final measurements: Approx 3 inches (7.6 cm) wide

5 Stitch the button to the center of the flower using your embroidery thread.

6 Sew the brooch pin to the back of the flower, and you're done!

Felt DAHLIA PIN

This is the perfect "lap project" to take on the go. If you're going to have some wait time sitting on the bus, at the airport, in the doctor's office, or any time you need a quick activity, this simple stitched-petal flower is all you'll need to keep boredom at bay (without resorting to the bottomless abyss of your cell phone screen). Before you know it, your wait will be over and you'll have a little pile of dahlias to show for yourself.

To make one flower:

1 strip of felt measuring 36 x 1 inches (91.4 x 2.5 cm)

1 strip of felt measuring 18 x 1 inches (45.7 cm x 2.5 cm)

1 square of felt measuring 2 x 2 inches (5.1 x 5.1 cm)

Perle cotton thread

1 button (vintage ones are nice for this project)

1 brooch pin measuring 1 inch (2.5 cm)

Embroidery needle

If you don't have felt yardage, you can cut pieces from a square of craft store felt totaling the same length. If any of your petals are larger than others, it's best to start with the larger ones and save the smaller ones for the inner layers. Irregularity in cuts happens, but imperfection can be charming!

assemble

Final measurements: 4 inches (10.2 cm) wide

make

1 Fold the 36 x 1-inch (91.4 x 2.5 cm) strip of felt in half and cut it every 1½ inches (3.8 cm) to make a pile of 24 larger rectangles. Cut a U shape out of each rectangle. These will be all of your petals. It's fine if the cuts are a little irregular, but if you're a

perfectionist, by all means take your time! Repeat this step with the second strip of felt, though cut this strip every 1 inch (2.5 cm) to cut out 18 smaller petals.

2 Cut a circle out of the small square of felt, taking care to waste as little material as possible. Cut up as close to that edge as you can.

3 Thread your needle with a length of perle cotton. Position the base of the first large petal at 9 o'clock on the felt circle base and stitch half the length of the base to secure it.

4 Half of your first larger petal should be stitched to the base, and the other half should be loose now because you just made one little stitch. Next, to add some dimension to the petal, fold the unstitched half of the petal base over to make a little pleat. Stitch the folded part of the petal to the base to secure it. Take a look at the assembly photo if you need a little help visualizing that. (I know I would!)

5 Continuing clockwise around the edge of the felt base, add the next large petal right on the pleat of the one before it. Stitch part of the petal base down, fold the other side over for dimension, and then stitch the fold down to secure the entire petal. Continue clockwise around the base, adding more large petals until the first layer is finished. So lovely!

6 For the next layer, fold in the edges of one petal to meet in the center. Holding the folded petal in one hand, position the petal on the flower base and stitch it in place. Keep folding petals and stitching them clockwise around the flower base until you finish that layer. It should be looking pretty fluffy by now.

7 Folding petals the same way as in step 6, use the remaining smaller petals you have to fill out the center of the flower.

8 Stitch your button to the center of the flower.

9 Sew the brooch pin to the back of the flower, and you're done!

Thistle
BOUTONNIERE

I've always thought of thistles as kind of a stoic flower. They're very angular and sturdy, with a sort of prickly determination. This decidedly noble flower makes a great simple boutonniere for a lady or gentleman.

To make one boutonniere:

1 piece of green wool felt measuring 5 x 1 inches (12.7 x 2.5 cm

1 wooden skewer (like the ones you use for barbecuing)

Purple wool roving

Gray wool roving

Dishwashing soap

1 fabric-covered 18-gauge floral wire measuring 3 inches (7.6 cm)

2 vintage millinery leaves

Floral tape

Baker's twine

Straight boutonniere pin

Pinking shears

Wire cutters

Bowl of very hot water

Bowl of very cold water

Hot glue gun

make

1 Trim one side of the 1-inch (2.5 cm) wide strip of green felt with pinking shears.

2 Use the wire cutters to snip a skewer to 3 inches (7.6 cm) long.

3 Tear a piece from your purple wool roving. You want enough to fit in your hand, roughly the size of a deck of cards.

4 Put a dab of soap in your hands and lightly handle the roving to get it just a little soapy. Gently form the roving into an airy ball shape and roll it in your hands a bit to get the soap on the wool.

assemble

Final measurements: Each bloom, approx ¾ inch (1.9 cm) wide

5 Dip the wool ball into your bowl of hot water just enough to get it damp, and continue to roll the wool in your hands to form a ball. As it takes shape, dip the ball into the bowl of cold water to "shock" the fibers and continue to shape the wool in your hands.

6 Keep alternating between hot and cold water as you roll the ball until it is very dense and the soap has been rinsed out. Set the ball on a towel to dry.

7 Wiggle the skewer into the base of your wool felt ball until it feels like it's about halfway into the ball. Secure it with a dab of glue at the base of the stem. Be neat about it, but don't worry about it showing, because it will be covered by the thistle leaves.

8 Glue the end of the narrow strip of green felt to the stem about ¾ inch (1.9 cm) down from the base of the flower and wind the strip around and up the skewer toward the flower base, securing the end with a dab of glue.

9 Pull a small piece of gray wool roving, smaller than you used for the thistle, and use the same felting technique to make a smaller ball.

10 Push the covered floral wire into the small gray ball until it just almost pokes through but not quite.

11 Arrange the thistle stem and the small gray flower together with the millinery leaves and wrap them together in floral tape.

12 Wrap baker's twine around the floral tape to cover it, and glue the end of the twine to the back of the boutonniere to secure.

13 Attach it to your lapel (or the lapel of one of your favorite people) with a boutonniere pin!

BURLAP
Hanging Flower

These giant poms look great in any setting from a rustic barn wedding to the high ceilings in your apartment. Any stiff, iron-friendly fabric can work for this technique, but I love upgrading a plain, underappreciated fabric like burlap into something so pretty and special.

gather

To make one flower:
100 (approximately) 6 x 6-inch (15.2 x 15.2 cm) burlap squares (Luckily, burlap is CHEAP!)

1 foam ball measuring 5 inches (12.7 cm)

1 piece of ribbon or twine measuring 12 inches (30.5 cm)

Iron

Straight pins

Hot glue gun

make

1 Fold your burlap as if you were making a paper snowflake: fold the square in half diagonally to make a triangle, then in half again so the pointy corners meet. Fold the pointed corners together again.

2 Iron the heck out of that little triangle. You want it to have lots of creases, which will add volume to your pompom later.

3 While the burlap is still folded, cut a wavy petal shape across the non-folded edge; it really is like a paper snowflake! Repeat with all of the burlap squares. Fall in love with the squares. Become one with making burlap snowflake flowers. Put on a little music; you're going to be here for a while

assemble

Final measurements: Approx 10 inches (25.4 cm) in diameter

4 Push a pin through the point where all the creases meet in the center of one of the burlap petals, and add a dollop of hot glue to the tip of the pin. Then push the pin into the foam ball to attach the petal to the surface.

5 Position your second petal close to the first one, so their petals almost hold each other up. (This is why you made so many!) Pin more petals all the way around the circumference of the foam ball. Keep working your way around the ball in a circular pattern until the ball is completely covered with your soft burlap petals.

6 Loop your ribbon in half, and push a pin through the ends into the top of the ball for hanging.

Really, you can make flower balls out of any flower. The foam ball center adds most of the oomph, and the straight pins make them easy to assemble. Felt Pom Flowers (page 21) or Felt Posy Flowers (page 26) would be the quickest and fluffiest. But, if you're feeling really ambitious (or if you're on bed rest or something and are going crazy wanting a project for your idle hands), you could even cover a ball in Embroidered Circle Flowers (page 44) and just blow everybody's minds with your craftiness.

EMBROIDERED FELT
Flower Pillow

Making a simple cover for a pillow is one of the easiest ways to add your individuality and taste to your home. They're as fun to design and create as they are to switch out, so make these in a few different color schemes, and you'll always have an easy way to freshen up your space. The flowers that adorn this fuzzy felt pillow cover can be easily made with felt scraps and pieces from other projects, so this is a great time to dig around in your stash for some creative color combinations!

To make one pillow case and nine flowers:

1 piece of 2-mm-thick wool or wool-blend felt measuring 15 x 29 inches (38.1 x 73.7 cm)

1 square pillow form measuring 14 inches (35.6 cm)—to be covered!

4 of your favorite decorative buttons

Cotton embroidery floss in your favorite colors

27 squares of wool felt measuring 3 x 3 inches (7.6 x 7.6 cm)

Straight pins

Crewel needle

Hand-sewing needle

Fabric-marking pen

Templates (page 127)

make

1 Fold the 15-inch (38.1 cm) edge of the felt about halfway up the length of the piece of fabric. Center your pillow on the felt to line up the folded edge with the center of the pillow. Pin the sides of the felt in place.

2 Place each of the four buttons along the folded edge of the felt and use the embroidery thread and crewel needle to stitch them in place.

3 Hand-stitch up the sides of the pillow cover to secure the bottom flap.

assemble

Final measurements: Each flower, approx 2½ inches (6.4 cm) wide; Pillow, 14 inches (35.6 cm) wide

4 Fold the top edge of the felt down to meet the buttons, and mark where the buttonholes should go with the fabric-marking pen. Carefully snip a ¾-inch (1.9 cm) slit on the top flap for each button.

5 Use the flower templates to cut out nine large, nine medium, and nine small flower shapes from your squares of felt. This is also a great time to use scraps and pieces from your stash because these flowers can be made with such small pieces!

6 Arrange the flowers with three layers each. Stitch each layer together using your favorite decorative embroidery stitches.

7 Finally, sew each of the nine flowers to the front of the felt pillow cover. Slide the pillow inside, button the flap down, and showcase your handiwork on your couch or bed, or just carry the pillow with you everywhere you go to show it off at all times.

CHERRY BLOSSOM
Push Pins

Real cherry blossoms are a very beautiful but short-lived bloom, making them a perfect pick for fabric reproduction. Making these extra special flowers out of felt lets you capture their prettiness without worrying about wilt. Display them on their own or use them as an unexpected addition peeking out of a felt flower bouquet.

To make one flower:
1 piece of felt measuring 5 x 1 inches
(12.7 x 2.5 cm)

Waxed thread

3 millinery stamens

Hand-sewing needle

Hot glue gun

Flat-head thumbtacks

Template (page 126)

make

1 Cut the strip of felt into five equal 1-inch (2.5 cm) squares.

2 Use the template as a guide to cut a cherry blossom petal shape out of each felt square. You can eyeball these pretty easily; simply cut a curve up each side of the piece, with the cuts meeting at the top to create a point. Snip a V-shaped notch in the tip of each petal. Irregularity is just fine. After all, real petals aren't identical either.

3 Thread your needle with a thin piece of waxed thread and sew a running stitch along the base of each petal. Leave a 3-inch (7.6 cm) tail of thread instead of moving the petals all the way to the end of the thread.

4 After each petal has been strung with a running stitch, gather the petals by tying the ends of the thread in a simple knot. Don't close the petals completely.

assemble

Final measurements: Each blossom, approx 2 inches (5.1 cm) wide

5 Insert the three millinery stamens through the center of the gathered flower. Once you get them in there, cinch the thread to close the flower and tie it tightly closed.

6 Next, fuss with the length of the stamens and snip off the excess underneath the flower. Put a dab of hot glue on the underside of the flower to secure the stamen wires. I like to cover the ends of the wires with a small scrap of felt just so the underside looks clean. Place the scrap right on there when the glue is still hot and hold the flower together for a moment to secure.

7 Use hot glue to secure the back of the cherry blossom to the head of a thumbtack. Once it has cooled, it'll look perfect on your corkboard!

FABRIC Blooms

CHIFFON FLOWER
Fairy Lights

Remember the super-easy (and crazy-pretty!) Felt Pom Flowers you made on page 21? This project puts a new spin on that tried-and-true basic fringe flower technique using some different materials. The soft, ephemeral loveliness of chiffon makes these flowers ideal for adorning strings of dreamy fairy lights. It's the perfect project to add a custom touch to a wedding party or create some romantic bedroom lighting.

gather

To make 50 flowers:
50 strips of silk chiffon measuring 12 x 1 inches (30.5 x 2.5 cm); just snip and rip! Rough edges will simply add to the effect.

150 millinery stamens

1 string of 50 clear indoor lights

Low-temperature hot glue

make

1 Fringe each strip of chiffon, snipping about every ½ inch (1.3 cm) as far down as you can without cutting all the way through. It'll save you time if you can snip through multiple layers at once, but don't rush yourself.

2 Hot glue three stamens around the plastic base of the first bulb.

3 Take one end of your fringed strip and use a dab of glue to secure it to the base of the bulb. Be sure not to get any glue on the bulb itself.

assemble

Final measurements: Each flower, approx 2 inches (5.1 cm) tall

4   Wrap the chiffon around the base of the bulb, adding a dab of glue every few rounds, until you get to the end. Secure with a final bit of glue.

5   Continue down the string. For softer light, cover every bulb with chiffon. You can also alternate between bare bulbs and flower ones for variety and to let more light shine through.

6   Hang your fairy lights where they can be best enjoyed! Don't forget to turn them off when you aren't in the room.

RUFFLY ROUND
Posy Garland

Experimenting with different petal shapes can change so much about a flower: swapping full circles for petal shapes results in full, fun little pompoms. These make a great garland for parties, or just hang them around your house for joyous décor every day!

To make 14 flowers:
112 felt circles measuring 2 inches
(5.1 cm)

Waxed thread

2 yards (1.8 m) of baker's twine

Crewel needle

make

1 Fold your first circle into quarters (fold in half, then in half again).

2 Thread your needle with the waxed thread and string the folded piece of felt onto the thread, pushing the needle through the corner of the folded circle.

3 Repeat steps 1 and 2 with seven more circles until you have a total of eight folded circles strung onto your waxed thread.

4 Tie the ends of the waxed thread, gathering all of the circles together. Tease them gently into a ball shape, allowing the circles to open up and reveal a very cool ruffled look. Tie off the thread and set the ball aside.

assemble

Final measurements: Each flower, approx 1¾ inches (4.4 cm) wide

5 Repeat steps 1 through 4 with the rest of the felt circles to create 14 ruffly felt flowers in total.

6 After finishing each ruffly flower, string them one by one onto the baker's twine. You can squish them all together or space them out according to your aesthetic.

Like all of the flowers in this book, these ruffly round flowers can also be stemmed, arranged into a bouquet, or plunked into a vase. Just hot glue a wrapped floral stem into the center!

Succulent WREATH

I love a beautiful handmade flower wreath to bring freshness to my space, but there's something even more inspiring about this lush and unusual velvet succulent wreath. I first learned about succulents in a wedding magazine I was reading as I planned my own nuptials, and the surprisingly floral shape of these pretty little plants makes them one of my favorite designs to work with.

To make 23 flowers:

Up to ½ yard (45.7 cm) total of light green and dark green velvet (Check the remnant sections at your favorite fabric store!)

Purple and/or magenta permanent markers

1 foam wreath base measuring 14 inches (35.6 cm); you can get wreath bases in all sort of shapes and sizes. A heart-shaped succulent wreath or three smaller wreaths connected with ribbon would be absolutely adorable!

Hand-sewing needle

Embroidery floss

Baker's twine or yarn (optional)

Hot glue gun

Straight pins

Note:

This wreath was made with a 14-inch (35.6 cm) base covered with 23 individual flowers. Each flower was made with 18 to 24 velvet petals, one coiled strip of velvet, and a circle of felt on the back. Depending on the diameter of your wreath base, you may need more or fewer flowers.

Final measurements: Each flower, approx 4 inches (10.2 cm) wide; Outer edge of wreath, 14 inches (35.6 cm) in diameter

make

1 For each succulent, cut a 9 x ½ inch (22.9 x 1.3 cm) strip of velvet and a 2-inch (5.1 cm) circle of green felt. Set these aside.

2 Each petal is made from a rectangle of velvet measuring 1½ x 1 inches (3.8 x 2.5 cm). If you're working with remnants of velvet, cut 18 to 24 rectangles from your fabric. If you're working with substantial pieces of velvet, try cutting a long 1½-inch (3.8 cm) wide strip of velvet and then snipping it into 1-inch (2.5 cm) rectangles.

3 Cut each of the pieces of velvet into a simple petal shape with a pointed top and wider bottom (almost like a curly bracket on your keyboard). See the assembly photo to understand how this should look.

4 If you'd like, add interest to the petals by coloring some of the edges of the velvet with permanent marker.

5 Fold the bottom corners of each petal into the center and use a dab of hot glue to secure them. Make sure that the majority of what is showing on your petal is the fluffy side of the velvet, not the smooth side.

6 Thread your needle with a length of embroidery floss. Position the first petal on the edge of the felt circle and stitch the petal's base to secure it. Continue stitching petals around the outside of the circle, being mindful not to leave any big spaces.

7 After you finish the first layer of petals, continue layering them atop the outer circle, working in toward the center. I usually stitch three layers of petals and add the occasional two or three petals to the center with hot glue if needed.

8 Coil the strip of velvet, using a small dab of hot glue to secure it. Glue it to the center of the succulent.

9 Repeat steps 1 through 8 until you have 23 succulents. You'll be making a lot of these, so feel free to experiment with color and size!

10 If you're using a foam wreath base and don't want the color to show through the flowers, wrap the wreath in baker's twine or yarn, securing both ends with hot glue.

11 Now you get to place your succulents! Using the straight pins, position your flowers. The nice thing about the pins is that you can change your mind.

12 When your wreath is sufficiently full, you can glue your succulents to make their placement permanent or keep in the pins so you can mix it up later.

SUMMMER FLOWER
Wreath

This tutorial is perfect for making a wreath that can be either hung on a wall or worn in your hair. Try experimenting with the size of the wire circle and the number of flowers to make a bigger or smaller wreath that can serve as anything from a huge decoration for your front door to a small bangle for your wrist!

To make 1 wreath:

6 Poppies (see page 42), make them from cotton fabric if you don't want to use raw silk

6 Pom Flowers (see page 21), made from fabric, not felt, for this project!

2 pieces of covered green floral wire measuring 18 inches (45.7 cm) each

Green floral tape

12 vintage millinery leaves

Green cotton yarn

2 small plastic hair combs (optional)

Wire cutters

Hot glue gun

make

1 With wire cutters, trim the stems of each flower to about 3 inches (7.6 cm)—you don't need such a long stem for this project.

2 Twist the two pieces of floral wire together into a circle to fit around your head. Use the green floral tape to cover the wires, and wrap the tape around the whole wreath to give the wire a nice sticky surface.

3 Arrange the flowers around the circumference of the wire and fuss with them until you like the look. When you're happy with the layout, wrap the stems of each flower around the wreath base to attach them

assemble

Final measurements: Approx 10 inches (25.4 cm) in diameter

securely. Keep working around the wreath, attaching the flowers by twisting the wires together until they're all secure around the circumference of the wreath.

4 Wrap the stems of the millinery leaves around the wreath between each flower. I like to position them sort of randomly so the leaves look like they're growing a little more naturally. Once you add each of the leaves to the wreath, cover the wires with floral tape.

5 Anchor the end of the green yarn to the underside of the wreath with a dab of hot glue, and wrap the yarn around the wreath to cover all of the floral tape. I do this in sections, using about 12 inches (30.5 cm) of yarn at a time.

6 If desired, attach the hair combs to each side of the wreath with a dab of hot glue, and wrap yarn between the teeth to secure them.

TEMPLATES

All of these templates are shown at 100% size.

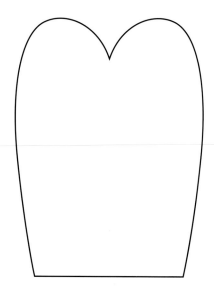

Band T-shirt Flower Pin
page 86

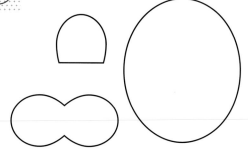

Bee & Blossom Sweater Clip
page 67

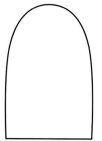

Cotton Dahlia Hair Clip
page 60

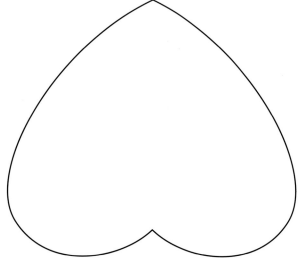

Calla Lily
page 28

Cherry Blossom Lapel Pin
page 88

Basic Rose
page 12

Soft Pink Rose Boutonniere
page 57

Embroidered Daisy
page 33

Felt Pom Flower
page 21

Silk Poppy
page 42

Jersey Posy Pin
page 65

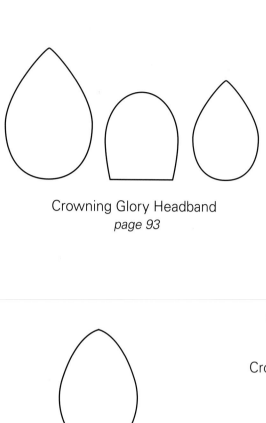

Crowning Glory Headband
page 93

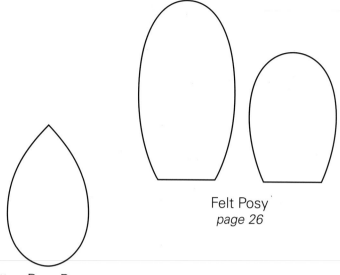

Felt Posy
page 26

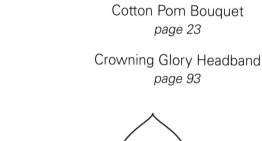

Cotton Pom Bouquet
page 23

Crowning Glory Headband
page 93

Silk Hydrangea
page 46

Felt Marigold
page 15

Cherry Blossom Push Pin
page 110

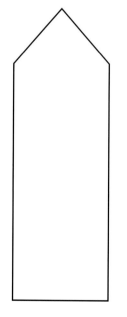

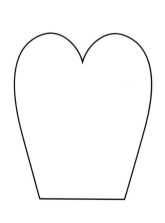

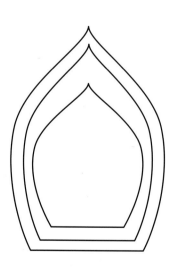

Sunflower Pin
page 90

Pleated Felt Headband
page 70

Poolside Posy Pin
page 54

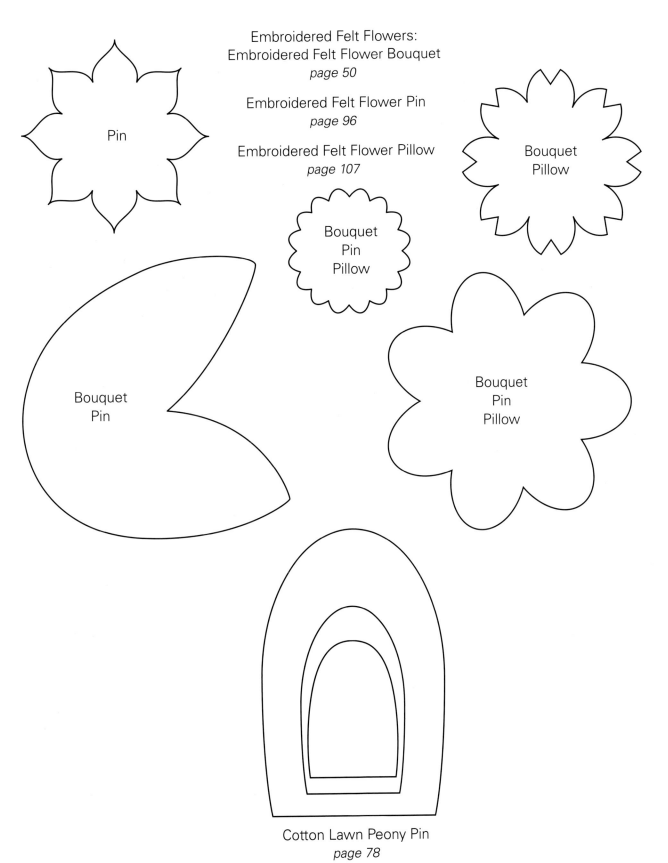

Pin

Embroidered Felt Flowers:
Embroidered Felt Flower Bouquet
page 50

Embroidered Felt Flower Pin
page 96

Embroidered Felt Flower Pillow
page 107

Bouquet
Pillow

Bouquet
Pin
Pillow

Bouquet
Pin

Bouquet
Pin
Pillow

Cotton Lawn Peony Pin
page 78

Credits

EDITORS
Beth Sweet
Amanda Carestio

ART DIRECTOR
COVER DESIGNER
Kathleen Holmes

ART PRODUCTION
Carol Barnao
Lisa Maddox

PHOTOGRAPHER
Justin Limoges

ILLUSTRATOR
Orrin Lundgren

About the Author

Megan Hunt is a bridal designer, freelance writer, and serial entrepreneur. She has spoken at conferences and in classrooms all over the country on such topics as entrepreneurship, women in business, industry techniques, and new-media magic. Megan lives in Omaha, Nebraska, where she devotes her time to civic activism and supporting local entrepreneurs and creatives. What she loves most about her job is meeting and collaborating with passionate people and being able to take her daughter, Alice, to work every day.

Acknowledgments

All of my thanks and love is owed to my longtime assistant and friend, Shannon Jackson. She has been the magic maker and lifesaver supporting my business goals and personal life for the last three years. Thank you for all of your chain stitches, all-nighters, and food runs. Thank you for all of the times you took care of my daughter so I could make it to a meeting or focus on finishing a project. Thank you for all of the kind notes left for me to find, for hassling me about meeting my deadlines, and for your endless positivity. You're a killer babe.

I'd like to thank Justin Limoges for his work on the photography for this book—thank you for always being available for re-shoots and thank you for your friendship. And of course, thanks to art director Kathy Holmes and designer Carol Barnao for taking all of my ideas and making it pretty, as I say.

I also want to give my gratitude to my mom, Mary Beth, for her unwavering support in my journey as a creative entrepreneur—you knew I was always meant to do this. Thanks to my business partner/life coach Sarah Lorsung Tvrdik and my hairdresser/spiritual advisor Rebecca Forsyth for your encouragement, and to authors Kari Chapin Nixon and Jo Packham for your example. Thanks, too, to my editor, Amanda, who probably had to put way more work into making this first book happen for me than she bargained for. More thanks to David Homan, my advisors Dusty Davidson and Dusty Reynolds, my travel agent Chris Guillebeau, and artist Watie White. You all know how much you have done for me as I worked to complete this project. Thank you.

Index